INTRODUCTION

The Blood Angels are the noblest of all the Space Marines. Though the Chapter harbours a sinister secret that dooms it to almost certain extinction, nowhere amongst the armies of Mankind can more valorous warriors be found, nor any more committed to the Emperor's dream and the survival of humanity.

The Warhammer 40,000 rulebook contains the rules you need to fight battles with your Citadel miniatures set in the war-torn universe of the 41st Millennium. Every army has its own Codex book that works alongside these rules, allowing you to turn your collection of miniatures into an organised force ready for your games of Warhammer 40,000. This Codex details everything you need to know about the Blood Angels Chapter of Space Marines.

WHY COLLECT A BLOOD ANGELS ARMY?

The Space Marines are the steadfast heroes of the Imperium. By their martial prowess and valour is Mankind preserved from extinction at the hands of a galaxy filled with unimaginable terrors. As one of the oldest and most revered of all Space Marine Chapters, the Blood Angels have stood at the forefront of humanity's defence for over ten thousand years. With bolter and chainsword they hold the foes of Mankind at bay in an unending battle for survival. Yet the Blood Angels are touched by a terrible flaw that threatens to undo their endless centuries of heroism, a dark madness that only strength of will can hope to contain.

The Blood Angels are the masters of war in all its forms, but they excel in the savage arena of close assault above all others. Every Battle-Brother feels the lure of hand-to-hand combat boiling in his blood – only eye-to-eye and blade-to-

blade with the foe can the dark beast within the Chapter's collective soul be given full reign. Caution is not the Blood Angels' way, and it cannot be yours. Assault Squads, Death Company, Sanguinary Guard – these are the spearhead of your host, but the rest of the army must follow close behind. Stormraven Gunships roar over the battlefield, bringing fresh troops into the maelstrom. Tactical Squads make their implacable advance, heavy weapons fire scouring the bastions of the foe, and tanks spur forward to spit death at the enemy from point blank range.

The Blood Angels are an army fit only for the boldest of generals. Do you have what it takes to lead them to victory?

HOW THIS CODEX WORKS

Codex: Blood Angels contains the following sections:

The Blood Angels: This section introduces the Blood Angels and their deeds in the Warhammer 40,000 universe. Included are the full details of their heritage, organisation and tales of the Chapter's greatest battles.

The Angelic Host: Here you will find a full examination of every character, squad and tank in the Blood Angels army. Firstly, you will find a full description of each unit, detailing its role within the army and its specialised combat abilities. Secondly, you will discover complete rules for the unit, as well as any details of unique skills, wargear or special abilities they can bring to bear against the foes of humanity.

This section also includes full details and rules for the unyielding armour and devastating weapons employed by the Blood Angels.

Warriors of Baal: This section contains colour photographs of the extensive range of Citadel miniatures available for your army, gloriously painted by Games Workshop's 'Eavy Metal team. Here you'll find examples of the colour schemes and heraldry used by the Blood Angels, as well as those used by their Successor Chapters.

Blood Angels Army List: The army list takes all the units presented in the Angelic Host section and arranges them so you can choose an army for your own games. Each unit type also has a points value attached to help you pit your forces against an opponent's in a fair match.

FIND OUT MORE

While Codex: Blood Angels contains everything you need to play a game with your army of Blood Angels, there are always more tactics to try, scenarios to fight and painting ideas to explore. The monthly White Dwarf magazine contains articles about all aspects of the Warhammer 40,000 game and hobby, and you can also find articles specific to the Blood Angels on our website:

www.games-workshop.com

BLOOD ANGELS

By Matthew Ward

CONTENTS

Art: John Blanche, Alex Boyd, Rob Carey, Paul Dainton, Dave Gallagher, Neil Hodgson, Nuala Kinrade, Adrian Smith. **Book Design:** Carl Dafforn, Emma Parrington, Mark Raynor. **Photography:** Glenn More, Ian Strickland. **'Eavy Metal:** Neil Green, Kornel Kozak, Darren Latham, Keith Robertson, Joe Tomaszewski, Anja Wettergren, Kirsten Williams, Tom Winstone. **Games Development:** Alessio Cavatore, Robin Cruddace, Graham Davey, Andy Hoare, Jervis Johnson, Phil Kelly, Andrew Kenrick, Jeremy Vetock, Matthew Ward. **Hobby Team:** Dave Andrews, Nick Bayton, Mark Jones, Chad Mierzwa, Chris Peach, Duncan Rhodes. **Miniature Design:** Mike Anderson, Giorgio Bassani, Trish Carden, Juan Diaz, Martin Footitt, Jes Goodwin, Colin Grayson, Mark Harrison, Alex Hedström, Matt Holland, Neil Langdown, Aly Morrison, Brian Nelson, Oliver Norman, Seb Perbet, Alan Perry, Michael Perry, Dale Stringer, Dave Thomas, Tom Walton. **Production & Reprographics:** Simon Burton, Chris Eggar, Marc Elliott, Talima Fox, Zaff Haydn-Davies, Kris Jaggers, John Michelbach, Melissa Roberts, Rachel Ryan, James Shardlow, Kris Shields, Ian Strickland, Madeleine Tighe. **Special Thanks to:** Rick Priestley, Alan Merrett, Tim Sawyer, Matthew Hutson, Pete Gosling.

Produced by Games Workshop

UK	NORTHERN EUROPE	NORTH AMERICA	AUSTRALIA
Games Workshop Ltd., Willow Rd, Lenton, Nottingham, NG7 2WS	Games Workshop Ltd., Willow Rd, Lenton, Nottingham, NG7 2WS	Games Workshop Inc, 6711 Baymeadow Drive, Suite A, Glen Burnie, Maryland, 21060-6401	Games Workshop, 23 Liverpool Street, Ingleburn, NSW 2565

BLOOD ANGELS

The Blood Angels have defended the Imperium from its very earliest days. Under the command of their great Primarch Sanguinius, the Blood Angels fought in the vanguard of the Great Crusade as the Emperor strove to reunite sundered Mankind, and stood again at his side through the Horus Heresy when dreams were made dust by Warmaster Horus' traitorous actions. Of the nine Space Marine Legions who stayed true to the Emperor, none battled so hard or suffered so much as the Blood Angels. They fought through the greatest killing fields of that galaxy-spanning civil war, their genetically-enhanced bodies and battle-hardened minds tested to the limit. Through fire and slaughter the Blood Angels came at last to the final conflict aboard Horus' Battle Barge, the tumultuous battle that left Sanguinius dead, the Emperor mortally wounded and the Blood Angels accursed.

Just as the Emperor's fall marked the beginning of a slow decay for the Imperium, so did Sanguinius' death at the Warmaster's hands usher in the slow degeneration of the Blood Angels. Proud and beauteous though the Blood Angels remained after the loss of their Primarch, something sinister had settled in their souls, a Red Thirst that could not be satisfied, a dark hunger that brought only insanity. Every Blood Angel knows that if death in battle does not take him then, sooner or later, the madness within his soul will, for it will manifest as a Black Rage that cannot be sated and ends only in death. Little wonder is it then that the Chapter has a reputation for assailing the foe at the closest of quarters, thinking little of their own safety and less of the odds of victory. For one of the Blood Angels, mortal peril is as nothing when compared to the threat of one's honour betrayed from within. Better a clean and righteous death in battle than the profane agonies of insanity.

It would have been easy for the children of Sanguinius to surrender to their dark urgings, to turn astray from the path set for them by Primarch and honoured Emperor, yet the Chapter has never lost faith nor fallen from grace. To this day, near ten thousand years since the death of their Primarch, the Blood Angels defend Mankind with all the vigour and ferocity they displayed in the time of Sanguinius. However, they are a dying Chapter, for each passing year Battle-Brothers succumb to the Red Thirst at an ever-increasing rate, or hurl themselves into hopeless battle so that they might escape its grasp.

It may well be that in the millennia to come the Blood Angels will be no more than a name in the histories of Mankind, a fading memory conjured up in tales of battle and songs of great deeds. Should this come to pass, the Blood Angels mean to ensure that their legend is remembered as one of heroism and service, that they might repay the trust of their Primarch and their Emperor, and serve as an example to Mankind in whatever bleak days lie ahead. So it is that the Blood Angels fight on against the enemies of the Imperium, holding the Red Thirst in check through sheer force of will. Whatever the Blood Angels' flaws, nowhere in the Imperium can truer servants of the Emperor be found.

ORIGINS OF THE BLOOD ANGELS

Like all the great Space Marine Legions, the Blood Angels were born from the dying flames of the Age of Strife. The risen Emperor had united the warring factions of Terra, yet his vision did not end with one mere planet, nor even with the solar system in which it lay. His goal was nothing less than the reunification of scattered Mankind, to bring the sundered worlds and realms of humanity under a single beneficent rule. To do this, he would need a mighty army, an army unlike any the galaxy had ever seen, an army whose warriors knew no other loyalty than to their Emperor, and whose bodies and minds were hardened to withstand unceasing war. So were the Space Marines created.

The Emperor had long ago refined the techniques of genetic manipulation, and he set these skills to work once again, forging twenty extraordinary super-warriors to be his generals in the coming campaign. Thus were born the Primarchs of the Space Marine Legions, incredible beings whose martial powers were to be second only to the Emperor himself.

Yet, as with all great labours, the genesis of the Space Marines did not go entirely according to design – the Emperor's plan for his Primarchs was to be undone even before it had properly begun. Without warning, the Primarchs disappeared, scattered throughout the galaxy by an unknown force.

The Great Crusade
Though the loss of the Primarchs was a bitter blow, the Emperor was not dismayed for long. The Primarchs themselves could not be recreated, but their genetic records remained, and from these the Emperor created the mighty Space Marine Legions – the armies he had always intended his Primarchs to lead. It was at the head of the Space Marine Legions that the Emperor began his Great Crusade in earnest. Setting out from Terra, the Emperor led the Space Marines on a glorious campaign that sought to restore Mankind to greatness. No foe could withstand the onslaught of the Great Crusade. Despots, aliens and Daemons all fell to the relentless advance of the Space Marine Legions, worlds previously enslaved and terrorised flocking willingly to the banner of the nascent Imperium.

It was in the course of the Great Crusade that the lost Primarchs were at last reunited with their Emperor, taking up their rightful places as the masters of the Space Marine Legions. No mere warriors were the Primarchs – they were also shrewd and canny leaders of men, under whose command the righteous might of the Space Marine Legions increased a hundredfold. So it was that the Great Crusade surged onwards as never before. New battlefronts opened up under the Primarchs' direction and worlds were reclaimed by the hundred, nay, by the thousand. Throughout it all, the Blood Angels and their Primarch, Sanguinius, fought at the Emperor's side, serving as honour guard to their beloved creator. Driven by fiery temperament, the Blood Angels swiftly earned a fearsome reputation as shock troops, which came to feed a rivalry between them and the World Eaters Legion. Yet, in truth, the Blood Angels were never as ferocious as the World Eaters, for the wise influence of Sanguinius tempered their bloodlust.

Though he was yet in the early days of his legend, Sanguinius was thought to be the noblest of the Primarchs and was ever deep in the Emperor's counsel. Even Horus, proud Warmaster of the Great Crusade and Primarch of the Luna Wolves, sensed a purity of spirit in Sanguinius that he could never match, a oneness with their 'father' that no other Primarch could ever hope to approach. Whilst many of his brothers fought the Great Crusade solely out of the joy of battle, Sanguinius fought to secure the golden era of peace and prosperity which would surely follow. His vision was the Emperor's, a hope of Mankind united in peace and prosperity. Alas, it was a vision not to be.

The Horus Heresy
Just as it seemed that the Emperor's dream could be fulfilled, the Great Crusade ended in the most terrible and unimaginable way. It came to pass that Horus, trusted Warmaster of the Great Crusade, turned his back upon the Emperor and embraced the shifting glories of the Chaos Gods. To him rallied near half of the armies of Mankind, including many of the Space Marine Legions. On what should have been the brink of a new age of glory, humanity was plunged into the bleakest civil war it had ever known. Untold billions of lives were sacrificed upon the altar of battle, every soul feeding the rapacious hungers of the Chaos Gods.

If the Great Crusade was Mankind's finest hour, then the Horus Heresy was surely its blackest. Brother fought brother, with quarter neither offered nor given. Heroes were slain, worlds burned and the Emperor's dreams of peace were shattered forever.

In the midst of this darkness, the Blood Angels never wavered, but held true at the Emperor's side. Sanguinius now stepped into the void left by Horus' desertion, assuming command of the Emperor's loyal forces. In doing so, he thrust the Blood Angels into the brutal forefront of the fighting. The rivalry with the World Eaters now escalated into bitter enmity as the two Legions found themselves serving different masters, and their confrontations were to be amongst the bloodiest and hardest fought of that bloodiest of wars. It is said that Horus hated and feared Sanguinius more than any of his brothers and wove many strategies to ensnare or slay him, though all failed.

The Final Confrontation

Yet for all the might of the Emperor, for every effort of Sanguinius and the remaining loyalist Primarchs, the forces of Horus drove all before them. In too short a time, the Emperor of Mankind was assailed within his great palace on Terra. With only a comparative handful of loyal warriors at his side, he confronted the host of Daemons, traitors and corrupted Space Marines that fought at the treacherous Warmaster's side. The Blood Angels led the defence of the Emperor's Palace, never once losing heart, despite the terrible odds stacked against them. Alongside their Battle-Brothers of the Imperial Fists Legion, the valorous yet overmatched soldiers of the Imperial Army and the grim Adeptus Custodes, the Blood Angels held the walls of that final bastion. Yet the war could not be won, or even survived, through defence alone.

In a final desperate gambit, the Emperor took the fight to Horus' great Battle Barge *Vengeful Spirit*, teleporting into the heart of the enemy stronghold with the Blood Angels and Imperial Fists at his side. Only Space Marines could have withstood the horrors of that Daemon-haunted starship, and even they were sorely pressed. Sanguinius was swiftly separated from his comrades and, so the legend tells, was brought through artifice before the treacherous Horus. In evil cunning, the Warmaster offered Sanguinius one final chance to renounce the Emperor, to join with Horus' inevitable victory – yet the Primarch of the Blood Angels held true, and refused. Thus rejected, Horus flew into a rage and attacked. Even at the peak of his powers Sanguinius could not have hoped to prevail against the monster Horus had become, and the Primarch was weary and wounded from his travails on Terra.

When the Emperor at last entered Horus' sanctum, he found his rebellious Warmaster standing above Sanguinius' broken, bleeding corpse. In the battle that followed, Horus was finally vanquished, though the Emperor too was cast down

near to death. There are many tales told of this final battle and, though the exact facts are long lost, one detail holds through all the recitations through all the millennia since. Despite the Emperor's great power, he could never have bested Horus had not the blade of Sanguinius wrought a chink in the Warmaster's armour.

The Aftermath

The Imperium was forever changed in the wake of Horus' defeat. No longer would the beneficent Emperor take a martial role in Mankind's defence, for his shattered body was now sustained only by the life-giving machineries of the Golden Throne.

The reconstruction of his empire and the final rout of the traitor forces would now fall to the surviving Primarchs, men such as Rogal Dorn of the Imperial Fists and Roboute Guilliman of the Ultramarines. Indeed, it was Guilliman who would have the greatest lasting effect upon the now-leaderless Blood Angels. Through the Codex Astartes – that great treatise on the restructuring and ordering of the Space Marines – Guilliman's legacy would reshape the Blood Angels Legion into the Chapters that defend the Imperium to this day.

Mankind had suffered, and the Imperium was nearly destroyed, yet the Blood Angels would bear the pain longer and more deeply than most. Sanguinius' death heralded the awakening of the Red Thirst, and its curse would change the nature of the Chapter forever.

THE ORDERING OF THE HOST

The Blood Angels were amongst the first Space Marines to adopt Roboute Guilliman's Codex Astartes. At first glance it might seem odd that a Legion so proud of its traditions and so high in the Emperor's favour would set aside its individuality, but the events of the Horus Heresy had shaken the Blood Angels to their core. The death of Sanguinius left no clear line of succession and factions within the Blood Angels swiftly polarised around potential candidates. In addition, the onset of the Flaw was slowly making its presence felt, further muddying the Legion's future. Ultimately, it was Azkaellon, sole survivor of the Sanguinary Guard, who drove the Blood Angels' destiny onwards. Arguing that of all the questions facing the Legion, how it should henceforth be ordered for battle was by far the least of their concerns, Azkaellon oversaw the division of the mighty Blood Angels Legion into the Chapters that endure today: the Blood Angels themselves, who maintain the old Legion's heraldry and traditions, the Flesh Tearers, the Angels Vermillion, the Angels Encarmine and the Angels Sanguine. What became of Azkaellon himself after this point is unrecorded, but his legacy lives on in the Chapters he created.

Chapter Organisation

The Blood Angels and their Successor Chapters adhere as closely to the Codex Astartes as the Flaw allows – they recognise the Codex's strictures to be merely another form of discipline which can be used to abate the worst excesses of the Red Thirst. Accordingly, each Chapter has a nominal strength of one thousand Battle-Brothers under arms, further divided into ten companies of roughly one hundred Space Marines each.

The 1st Company is home to the Chapter's most experienced veterans; all of its Battle Brothers steeped in decades, if not centuries, of constant warfare. The 2nd through 5th Companies are the Chapter's backbone, the Battle Companies who form the core of any strike force, and bear the greatest burden in any campaign. The remaining companies are reserve and training formations of one sort or another. Companies 6 and 7 are the Tactical Companies, used to reinforce a strike force or battleline when the Battle Companies are overstretched. The 8th and 9th Companies are specialist formations, composed of Assault Squads and Devastator Squads respectively. These companies are rather more limited in their tactical scope than the others and are deployed only when an overwhelmingly single-minded approach is required. Finally, the 10th Company is seen by many as the future of the Chapter, for it is here that Scouts hone their skills in the Space Marine way of war. Of all a Chapter's companies, it is the 10th that fights least commonly as a single unit. Though the Scouts are not yet as deadly as fully-trained Space Marines, their skills are highly valued and, as a result, every strike force will likely have a squad or two of Scouts attached to it.

Though each company can, and does, fight as a separate unit, a Blood Angels strike force will often be composed of several squads from different companies, assembled on an ad hoc basis according to the mission at hand. Such strike forces are normally given code names, such as *Bloodspear*, *Liberator* or *Primarch's Wrath*. Nonetheless, a strike force will inevitably be referenced by the company from which most of its personnel are drawn, or the officer that leads it, such as *Strike Force Machiavi* (named for the officer in command). The Blood Angels admire a martial metaphor as much as the next Space Marine, but prize simplicity of association at least as highly.

In addition to the personal armour and weaponry required by its Battle Brothers, each company, save the 10th, also maintains a host of support vehicles, ranging from Rhino and Razorback transports to bikes and Land Speeders – such tools are drawn upon whenever the tactical situation requires. So it is that even a single Blood Angels company can fulfil a multitude of tactical and strategic roles. Unusually for a Space Marine Chapter, the Blood Angels are fortunate enough to command sufficient Land Raiders to deploy these mighty vehicles as line transports, rather than elite support units. How the Blood Angels acquired so many Land Raiders is something of a mystery outside the Chapter. Perhaps they were simply fortunate to have more survive the dark days of the Horus Heresy, or perhaps the Blood Angels were once closer allies of the Adeptus Mechanicus and thus far better postioned to replace their losses than other Chapters.

Chapter Command

Rule of the Blood Angels falls to the Chapter Master and his council. Most seats at the high table are taken by the Brother Captains who command the Chapter's companies. Some, however, are taken by senior officers whose injuries have become too great for them to pursue an active battlefield role, but whose wisdom still holds great value. Such officers command the Chapter's vital support institutions, such as the armoury, the fleet and the ongoing recruitment of fresh neophytes.

Though ultimate power rests with the Chapter Master, the council are often called upon to act in their master's absence should he be slain or is himself away on campaign. In addition to their role on the council, each officer will also have an assigned title and duties necessary for the smooth running of the Chapter. Some such titles, such as Master of the Watch, are drawn from the pages of the Codex Astartes. Others, including the Lord of Skyfall and the Shield of Baal, have sprung from the Blood Angels' unique nature.

It should be noted that unlike most other Codex Chapters, the Blood Angels Sanguinary Priesthood (the Blood Angels Apothecaries) and Reclusiam are also part of the Chapter Command, rather than subordinate organisations as would normally be the case. This structure means that the Sanguinary High Priest and High Chaplain take joint temporary rule in the event of the Chapter Master's death, rather than the rank automatically passing to the Captain of the 1st Company. This tradition arose during .M35, when Captain Kalael rose to the rank of Chapter Master and succumbed almost immediately to the Black Rage, throwing the Blood Angels into a spiritual and organisational crisis. By holding temporary command, the High Chaplain and Sanguinary High Priest can test the will and worthiness of the new candidate to ensure that such a rash and unfortunate appointment does not occur again.

Represented here is the composition and deployment of the Blood Angels Chapter circa 999.M41. For logistical reasons, each squad is assumed to have a nominal strength of ten Battle-Brothers, although battlefield attrition and instability brought on by the Flaw inevitably reduces this tally. In addition to the forces shown here, each company or strike force will also have a Death Company, although this is considered to be an auxiliary force. The Death Company's strength varies according to the onset of the Black Rage, and it therefore does not appear as an 'official' fighting body.

SANGUINARY PRIESTHOOD
Brother Corbulo
Sanguinary High Priest

21 Sanguinary Priests

CHAPTER MASTER
Commander Dante
Master of the Blood Angels,
Lord of the Angelic Host

RECLUSIAM
High Chaplain
Astorath the Grim
Redeemer of the Lost

13 Chaplains

SANGUINARY GUARD
Brother Sepharan,
Exalted Herald of Sanguinius

29 Sanguinary Guards

LOGISTICIAM
Brother Adanicio
Warden of the Gates

900 Chapter Equerries and Servitors

ARMOURY
Brother Incarael
Master of the Blade

35 Techmarines
105 Servitors
20 Predators
18 Baal Predators
5 Vindicators
7 Whirlwinds
43 Land Raiders
51 Stormraven Gunships

FLEET COMMAND
Brother Bellerophon
Keeper of the Heavengate

7 Strike Cruisers
2 Battle Barges
(Blade of Vengeance, Bloodcaller)
16 Rapid Strike Vessels
36 Thunderhawk Gunships
3 Thunderhawk Transporters

LIBRARIUS
Chief Librarian Mephiston

6 Epistolaries
11 Codiciers
8 Lexicanum
5 Acolytum
5 Furioso Librarian Dreadnoughts

1ST COMPANY
"Archangels"
Veteran Company
Captain Karlaen
Shield of Baal

101 Veterans
5 Furioso Dreadnoughts

2ND COMPANY
"The Blooded"
Battle Company
Captain Aphael
Master of the Watch

6 Tactical Squads
2 Assault Squads
2 Devastator Squads
3 Dreadnoughts

3RD COMPANY
"Ironhelms"
Battle Company
Captain Machiavi
Master of Sacrifice

6 Tactical Squads
2 Assault Squads
2 Devastator Squads
4 Dreadnoughts

4TH COMPANY
"Knights of Baal"
Battle Company
Captain Castigon
Lord Adjudicator

6 Tactical Squads
2 Assault Squads
2 Devastator Squads
4 Dreadnoughts

5TH COMPANY
"Daemonbanes"
Battle Company
Captain Sendini
Keeper of the Arsenal

6 Tactical Squads
2 Assault Squads
2 Devastator Squads
3 Dreadnoughts

6TH COMPANY
"Eternals"
Tactical Company
Captain Raxiatel
Caller of the Fires

10 Tactical Squads
3 Dreadnoughts

7TH COMPANY
"Unconquerables"
Tactical Company
Captain Phaeton
Master of the Marches

10 Tactical Squads
1 Dreadnought

8TH COMPANY
"Bloodblades"
Assault Company
Captain Zedrenael
Lord of Skyfall

10 Assault Squads
1 Dreadnought

9TH COMPANY
"Sunderers"
Devastator Company
Captain Sendroth
Master of Sieges

10 Devastator Squads
2 Dreadnoughts

10TH COMPANY
"Redeemers"
Scout Company
Captain Borgio
Master of Recruits

10 Scout Squads
56 Unassigned
Neophytes

PLANET OF THE BLOOD ANGELS

The Blood Angels are shaped not only by the personality and deeds of Sanguinius, but also by the nature of their Chapter planet, Baal. Few worlds in the entire Imperium could have as devastating an impact on the human soul as Baal and its inhabited moons: Baal Prime and Baal Secundus.

In ancient days Baal and its moons all had earth-like atmospheres. Baal itself was a world of rust-red deserts but its moons were paradises for mortal men, where folk lived in harmony with nature and pursued lives of ease and freedom. The people of Baal became exceptional artisans, and spent their time creating mighty monuments, carving the mountains themselves into statues of their rulers and their gods. They even ventured onto the surface of desolate Baal itself leaving colonies and breathtaking edifices in their wake.

No one knows exactly what happened to change this idyllic state of affairs. All that is certain is that during the fearful events that marked the downfall of human society and the end of the Dark Age of Technology, the moons of Baal suffered terribly. Ancient weapons of terrifying potency were unleashed. Cities became plains of smouldering glass. Lush grasslands became polluted deserts. Seas became poisoned lakes of toxic sludge. The people of Baal died in their millions and it looked as if humanity might become extinct in the Baal system. But somehow people survived. They clung precariously to life on the edges of the radioactive deserts. They became scavengers, picking through the scattered bones of their own once-great civilisation. In the dark time that followed the collapse of all order, some became worse than scavengers, and in their desperation turned to cannibalism.

Over the course of the following centuries, the accumulated chemical and radioactive toxins that built up in the survivors' bodies led to them devolving into mutants, shambling parodies of the men their forefathers had once been. There were some who held on to their humanity and preserved a semblance of sane behaviour, but these were the embattled few amongst a new and savage culture that evolved amid the ruins of the old. The only social unit left was the tribe. For human and mutant cannibal alike, the only folk they could rely upon were their own kin. The people of the Baal system became nomads, shifting from place to place, picking the ruins clean, warring to preserve the spoils they had gathered. The tribes fought constant wars, webs of alliances shifting constantly as each tribe strove for supremacy and survival. Extinction awaited the slow and the weak. Where once the moons had been near paradise, now they were living hells.

For the few surviving humans, existence was a constant struggle. They wandered the surface in ramshackle vehicles, desperately hoping that their patched-together radiation suits would save them, praying that they would never hear the hideous tell-tale clicking of their rad-counters, a sound that meant death was imminent. For a time it seemed that humanity was doomed and soon there would only be an endless desert ruled over by the feuding mutant tribes. Then, out of the star-strewn darkness of the heavens, came a sign of hope.

THE COMING OF SANGUINIUS

It happened that after the Emperor created the Primarchs, the infants were stolen from the chamber in which they lay. The forces of Chaos made off with the infants and carried them through the Warp. Unable to destroy the Primarchs because of the powerful protections laid on them by the Emperor, the daemonic powers nonetheless did their best to alter and mould the Emperor's work to their own evil ends. Thus it was that even the best of the Emperor's creations became corrupted at the outset.

The pod that housed the infant Sanguinius came to rest upon the surface of Baal Secundus, at the place now known as Angel's Fall. The infant Primarch was found by one of the wandering tribes of humans who called themselves the Folk of Pure Blood, or simply the Blood. The young Sanguinius' life almost came to an end then and there, for the touch of Chaos had changed him. Tiny vestigial wings, like those of an angel, emerged from his back. Many wanted to kill the child as a mutant, while others wanted to absolve the boy, for in all other ways he was as perfect a child as had ever been seen. Eventually innate compassion prevailed and the child was spared.

The infant Sanguinius was a prodigy – he grew quickly and learned everything his parents could teach him. After three weeks Sanguinius was as large as a child of three years. It is said that at this age he slew a giant fire scorpion with no weapon other than his bare hands, and that he never once showed fear at the colossal beast's onset. As Sanguinius grew his wings grew also, changing from tiny vestigial things into mighty pinions that could bear him aloft upon the desert air. By the time he was a year old, he looked and acted like a man in his youthful prime. He could walk without a rad-suit in the most poisonous of Baal Secundus' deserts, and could shatter massive boulders with a single blow of his outstretched hand. In the use of all weapons he soon excelled his teachers.

When a wandering band of mutants surprised the tribe, Sanguinius slew them all, although they numbered over a hundred. This was the first time the members of the Blood had ever seen him truly angry, for he felt his comrades' lives were in danger. When the blood-rage overtook him, Sanguinius was indeed terrible to behold – his mighty Primarch powers awoke to fullness and a nimbus of light played about his head.

Sanguinius distinguished himself in the fateful days and years that followed. He soon rose to leadership of the Blood, and under his guidance they rolled back the mutant tide. For a time Mankind had a respite on the moon of Baal Secundus. Sanguinius was worshipped as a god by his followers who felt that he could once again create a paradise in that dreadful land.

It was shortly thereafter that fate intervened once more. The Emperor had been questing across the galaxy in search of his lost children and his incredible psychic powers led him to Baal. His ship landed at the Conclave of the Blood, and he walked straight to Sanguinius' abode.

Some amongst the Primarchs are said to have fought against the Emperor when first they met but this was not the case with Sanguinius. He immediately recognised the Emperor for who he was and bent his knee before the Lord of Mankind. The Emperor raised him up and looked upon his people and saw that they were fair and noble. The best of the warriors he offered to raise up into Space Marines. The others were to be honourably left behind to defend Mankind's birthright upon Baal Secundus. The Emperor performed the complex operation that would extract the gene-seed from Sanguinius' genetic codes and he implanted it into the warriors of the Blood Angels Legion. Thus were the Blood Angels and their Primarch finally made whole. They joined the Emperor's fleet and sailed across the Sea of Stars to participate in the Great Crusade.

THE CREATION OF ANGELS

Since the time of Sanguinius, the Blood Angels have recruited from among the greatest tribes of the Blood on Baal Secundus and Baal Prime (where a colony was established shortly after the time of the Horus Heresy). Youths from the Blood take part in great games and tournaments, facing many hazards as they race across the desert, to fight and do battle against one other. These contests are usually held only once per generation at Angel's Fall, where a mighty statue of Sanguinius now observes the proceedings.

Traditionally, the Time of Challenge is announced by heralds who visit each tribe in great flying chariots. Contestants must make their way to Angel's Fall across the rad-deserts, a process that in and of itself weeds out the weakest, for the hazards of the desert are many, and it takes a youth of extraordinary skill and courage to even reach the Place of Challenge. Once there they must vie for the fifty or so places that are available. Those who succeed are taken up in Sky Chariots; those who fail are left behind either to guard the place of testing or to make their way back to their own tribes as they choose.

Those youths who are accepted as Aspirants are taken to the Blood Angels' fortress monastery on Baal itself. There they see great wonders and look for the first time on the unmasked faces of their future Brother Marines, and possibly note with some consternation their sharp eye-teeth and sleekly beautiful features. It has to be said that the recruits are far from handsome at this stage. Most of the Aspirants bear marks of their hard lives, for it is all but impossible for an ordinary man to dwell on those barren moons and not feel the terrible kiss of radiation. Many are marked by stigmata, most are short and stunted, their growth stifled by malnutrition and constant hunger. Many more will be marked by lesions and carcinoma.

All the Aspirants are left to observe vigil in the great Chapel of the Chapter and then they will drink from the Sanguinary Chalice brought to them by the Sanguinary Priest. They are told that they partake of the blood of their Primarch and

they drink. Slumber soon overtakes them and the aspirants are borne by Servitors to the Apothecarion where the gene-seed of Sanguinius will be implanted in their recumbent bodies. From the Apothecarion the aspirants will be taken to the Hall of Sarcophagi and each will be placed within a mighty golden sarcophagus. Life support nodes are attached to them and for the next year they will be fed intravenously with a mixture of nutrients and the Blood of Sanguinius while the gene-seed does its work.

Many die at this stage, their bodies unable to cope with the strain of the changes that now overtake them. Those who live will grow swift and true, echoing the rapid growth of their Primarch. They will put on muscle mass and acquire the extra internal organs that mark a true Space Marine. At this time too they will have many strange dreams, for the gene-seed carries within it many of the memories of Sanguinius. Thus will the essence of their Primarch begin to permeate the souls of his chosen warriors. Ever afterwards, when sleeping, and sometimes when awake, these dreams will return to haunt the future Blood Angels.

When the Aspirants emerge from their sarcophagi they are forever changed. They will be tall, strong and superhumanly powerful. Their restructured bodies and features will have taken on a beauty that echoes that of their angelic forebear. Their senses will be keener, their muscles will be stronger than tempered steel. They will be ready to begin their training as Space Marines.

THE HERITAGE OF SANGUINIUS

Sanguinius was a visionary. During his earliest life he desired to lead his people to a new and better life. When he joined the Great Crusade he did not abandon this vision, but instead brought it to a greater arena. He wanted a better life for all Mankind and an end to the strife brought on by the collapse of human civilisation at the close of the Dark Age of Technology.

Yet Sanguinius was not merely blessed with a futurist philosophy, he was also gifted with the power of prophecy, able to see visions of what lay ahead. It is almost certain that he knew he was going to his death when he boarded Horus' Battle Barge and yet he went anyway. Whether Sanguinius did this out of fatalism or loyalty to the Emperor is a point often debated by Imperial theologians, but it is not in doubt among the Blood Angels. They will say that he went out of duty, knowing full well what the outcome would be.

The outlook of Sanguinius did much to shape his Chapter. There is a powerful mystical streak to many of the Blood Angels' traditions, and this can only have come from the spiritual teachings of the winged Primarch. Sanguinius also indoctrinated his followers with a strong belief that things can be changed for the better. After all, the process of transforming a scabby scavenger into a tall, proud and handsome warrior is living proof of the tenet that courage, refinement and nobility can be shaped from the crudest clay.

This belief can be seen in all things the Blood Angels do – they strive for perfection. Their works of art are things of beauty. Their martial disciplines are practised unceasingly. As the Flaw within their gene-seed has become more evident, this belief in change has turned into an altogether darker thing. They also see evidence of Mankind's capacity for folly and destruction. Their doctrines are permeated with a sense of mortality and the fallen greatness of man.

Physically the Blood Angels are among the longest lived of all the Space Marine Chapters. One of the peculiarities of their aberrant gene-seed is that it has vastly increased the lifespan of those who bear it, so it is not uncommon for Blood Angels to live for a thousand years. Indeed, the current Commander of the Chapter, Dante, is known to have lived for 1,100 years, and is almost certainly far older. These vastly extended lifespans allow the Blood Angels to perfect their techniques in art as well as in war. They have centuries in which to perfect the disciplines to which they turn their minds. This accounts for the fact that the Blood Angels' armour and banners are amongst the most ornate of all the Space Marines.

Perhaps the strangest of all the Chapter's traditions is the habit of sleeping whenever possible in the sarcophagi used to create them. In recent years the Sanguinary Priests have created filters that purify the blood of their Brother Space Marines. While the Blood Angels sleep in their sarcophagi their blood is cleansed and purified. The Chapter thus hopes to slow the process of degeneration brought on by the Flaw.

THE FLAW

Although it is known to but a few, the Blood Angels are a dying Chapter, for they suffer from a dreadful flaw. This Chapter, once the most golden and blessed of all the Chapters, now shuns the company of its fellows where possible. Some, it is said, are driven by a terrible death-seeking madness, brought on by visions of the death of their Primarch. Others are afflicted by the terrible Red Thirst, a craving for blood which some claim may be the first signs of a descent into Chaos. It is known that some amongst the Blood Angels themselves spend much time seeking a cure for this condition, although most have resigned themselves to the slow and terrible decline of their Chapter.

Some say that it is because Sanguinius was more touched by Chaos than the others during his flight through the Warp. They cite the fact that he possessed wings – an obvious mutation – to support their case. Their argument runs that the gene-seed that was extracted from him was flawed even before the first Blood Angels were created, and thus terrible consequences were preordained. Others deny this, citing that the Emperor himself trusted the winged Primarch implicitly, and oversaw the creation of the Blood Angels. Certain heretics counter this with the argument that the Emperor also trusted Horus…

Other scholars claim that the Flaw lies in the process that is used to create each new generation of Blood Angels. They assert that it has crept in through the generations because the Blood Angels use the process known as Insanguination to activate the gene-seed.

All Space Marine Chapters use gene-seed to trigger and control the processes that transform an ordinary mortal into a Space Marine. The gene-seed is encoded with all the information needed to reshape ordinary cell clusters into the special organs Space Marines possess. The gene-seed contains viral machines which rebuild the body according to the biological template contained within it. However, even from the beginning, there was never a set way to activate the gene-seed.

Indeed, at the time when the Space Marine Legions were created, the process was still highly experimental and many different ways of controlling and managing the transformation were tried. This led to the Space Wolves using the ritual known as Blooding, the Imperial Fists using the process known as the Hand of Faith, the White Scars conducting the Rites of the Risen Moon and the Blood Angels using Insanguination.

The process of Insanguination was originally triggered by injecting the Aspirants with tiny samples of their Primarch's own blood. This practice, of course, ended with the tragic death of Sanguinius. However, some of his blood was kept and preserved within the Red Grail. The living blood could not be kept this way for long and so it was injected into the veins of the Sanguinary Priests. In this way they became living hosts to the power of Sanguinius. To this day, the drinking of the collected blood of the assembled Sanguinary Priests from the Red Grail is part of the induction ritual for all Blood Angels Priests.

It is from these Sanguinary Priests that blood is taken to begin the transformation of Aspirants into Space Marines. It is possible that over the countless generations since the time of the Horus Heresy these cells have mutated, slowly at first but more quickly in recent years, and that errors in replication have resulted in the Flaw.

Whatever the reason for the Flaw, it is certain that its hold over the Blood Angels has become ever stronger, and their tendency towards self-destructive madness ever greater. Unless it can be halted and reversed, the Chapter is doomed to extinction.

THE RED THIRST
Deep within the psyche of every Blood Angel is a destructive yearning, a battle fury and blood-hunger that must be held in abeyance in every waking moment. Few Battle-Brothers can hold this Red Thirst in check unceasingly – it is far from unknown for Blood Angels to temporarily succumb to its lure at the height of battle.

The Red Thirst is the Blood Angels' darkest secret and greatest curse, but it is also their greatest salvation, for it brings with it a humility and understanding of their own failings which make them truly the most noble of the Space Marines.

The fate of those unfortunates overtaken completely by the Red Thirst is known only to the Chapter itself. There are tales of a secret chamber atop the Tower of Amareo on Baal, and of howling cries that demand the blood of the living, but none are willing to say for certain what secrets lie hidden in this haunted, desolate place.

There have been incidents when the Blood Angels have been stationed on distant worlds where members of the local population have gone missing only to turn up later drained of blood. It is possible that this is the work of cultists seeking to discredit the Chapter. It may even be that some of the more superstitious local citizens have taken to offering up sacrifices to their god-like visitors. It may also be possible that these folk have been killed by Blood Angels overcome by the Red Thirst.

THE BLACK RAGE
Blood Angels are unique amongst the Space Marines in that deeply engrained in their gene-seed is the encoded experience of their Primarch, and most deeply imprinted of all is the memory of Sanguinius' final battle with Horus. Sometimes, on the eve of battle, an event or circumstance will trigger this 'race memory' and the Battle-Brother's mind is suddenly wrenched into the distant past. The Black Rage overcomes the Blood Angel as the memories and consciousness of Sanguinius intrude upon his mind, and dire events ten thousand years old flood into the present. A warrior overcome with the Black Rage appears half mad with fury; he is unable to distinguish past from present and does not recognise his comrades. He may believe he is Sanguinius upon the eve of his destruction, and the bloody battles of the Horus Heresy are raging all around him. Such a Battle-Brother stands at the end of his travails, for his path leads only to the Death Company, where he and the Chapter's other damned souls will fight one final battle in Sanguinius' name.

A LEGEND FORGED OF BLOOD

Few Space Marine Chapters are as prolific in their defence of the Imperium as the Blood Angels. Whilst Chapters such as the Ultramarines stand guard over particular systems or sectors, the Blood Angels see the whole Imperium as their responsibility. This has, on occasion, caused the Battle-Brothers of the Chapter to be spread rather thinly, and goes some way to explain the rather high rate of attrition amongst the Blood Angels' ranks. Nevertheless, the Blood Angels' battle record is deemed one of the most honourable in the Imperium, and their fame has spread far and wide. The events listed on the following pages are those that the Blood Angels themselves consider worthy of special celebration or commemoration.

746.M41 The Scouring of Ultramar.
Recognising that the Tyranid invasion of Ultramar is but the first of many yet to occur, Commander Dante sends three companies of Blood Angels to assist the Ultramarines in scouring the remaining beasts from the eastern sectors. Upon their return three years later, the three companies are much reduced in number, but wealthy in invaluable Tyranid-hunting doctrines that are swiftly passed on to the rest of the Chapter.

798.M41 The Assault on Baal.
Three colossal space hulks drop out of Warp in the Baal system, signalling the arrival of Waaagh! Big Skorcha. Dante orders the deployment of two companies to each of Baal's moons. The remaining companies are assigned to strike forces and ordered to board and destroy the space hulks. Two of the space hulks are destroyed with much of the Waaagh! still on board.

Before it too is destroyed, the final space hulk disgorges thousands of Orks, the Warlord Big Skorcha among them, onto the surface of Baal. Knowing the bulk of the Blood Angels forces to still be in orbit or on the two moons, Big Skorcha aims to breach and ransack the Chapter's Fortress Monastery. However, the Blood Angels are not to be so easily outmanoeuvred.

The Chapter's Dreadnoughts, deemed unsuitable for the Space Hulk assaults, had remained in battle readiness on Baal itself. With the remains of Waaagh! Big Skorcha on the loose, Venerable Furioso Astramael assembles all forty-one of the Chapter's functional Dreadnoughts and coordinates the defence of the Fortress Monastery in what will later come to be known as the Battle of Iron. Although Astramael needed only to defend the Fortress Monastery long enough for reinforcements to arrive from orbit, such was the fury with which he prosecuted the brief, but bloody, campaign, there were precious few Orks remaining when the first Stormravens landed.

801.M41 Assault of Kammelstadt.
Captain Zorael leads strike force *Bloodhawk* against insurrectionist rebels on Golgotha. Taking to their Land Raiders, the Blood Angels form an armoured column and smash through the outer fortress walls. Trapped behind their own defences, the rebels are swiftly overwhelmed by Zorael's Stormraven Gunships.

802.41 Reign of Blood.
The Blood Drinkers Chapter come to the aid of the Cadian 35th as they lay siege to the Daemon-infested hive world of Helios Alpha. The Blood Drinkers' ferocious assault swiftly breaks the stalemate, although the high incidence of collateral damage amongst the Guardsmen fighting alongside the Blood Drinkers leaves Cadian High Command decidedly hesitant to accept the Chapter's aid again.

815.M41 A New Beginning.
Gabriel Seth becomes Master of the Flesh Tearers. His first act is to repair relations between his Chapter and the Blood Angels, the pact of brotherhood having been sundered by centuries of the Flesh Tearers' bloodthirsty ways.

820.M41 Bloodcaller's Triumph.
The Blood Angels Battle Barge *Bloodcaller* is badly damaged by an Ork pirate ambush whilst on a patrol of the Tresinka system. With its main drives all but silent, boarding Kroozers clamped to its flanks and Orks loose in its belly, the *Bloodcaller* seems doomed.

Nonetheless, deft manoeuvres by Fleet Captain Bellerophon bring the mighty vessel's main batteries to bear on the greenskin fleet, obliterating the flagship and half a dozen support vessels in a single salvo. Meanwhile, the furious counterassault by *Bloodcaller*'s crew sweeps the Ork boarding parties from the Battle Barge's decks and carries the fight into the Kroozers. Though it takes a year for the *Bloodcaller* to limp to the Imperial Fleet repair docks at Haringvleet, it does so proudly bearing the scars of a great victory won against incredible odds.

823.M41 The Khartas Incident.
Captain Zorael of the 4th Company is slain by the Bloodthirster Ka'Bandha. Only the intercession of the Sanguinor prevents total destruction of Zorael's strike force. Francesi Castigon becomes Captain of the 4th Company.

830.M41 The Axonar Spirewar.
Dante sends the 3rd and 4th Companies to quell rebellion on the hive world of Axonar. Deeming the defences at the base of the hive cities to be too formidable for a direct assault, Captain Metraen orders a series of low-orbit jump pack insertions onto the upper spires. Trapped behind their own defences, the rebels are swiftly crushed.

843.M41 The Dalaric Campaigns.
Three Companies of Blood Angels are sent to Dalaric in order to halt the predations of the perfidious Eldar. A series of victories is all but swept away by a disastrous ambush in which the Eldar slaughter more than a hundred Battle-Brothers. Fortunately, in the darkest hour, the Sanguinor appears, striking down the alien Avatar and driving the surviving Eldar to flight.

859.M41 Assault on Ice Planet Zoran.

The Alpha Legion incite an uprising on the frozen planet Zoran. Blood Angels Captain Metraen leads elements of the 3rd and 8th Companies to crush the insurrection and drive the Traitor Legion from the planet. Metraen's impetuous tactics initially dictate the course of the battle, but the attack stalls when the Alpha Legion's base of operations is discovered to be nothing less than an ancient Imperator Titan. Though half-buried in the ice, the behemoth's void shield generators and weapons batteries are still fully operational. Many Battle-Brothers fall in the first assault and Metraen fears he may have to resort to Exterminatus.

Fortunately, help unlooked for arrives in the shape of Kor'sarro Khan and the White Scars 3rd Company. Sent to claim the head of the Alpha Legion's Lord Voldorius, the Khan swiftly joins forces with the dwindled Blood Angels. As the White Scars assail the fortress from below, the Blood Angels take to the skies in their Stormravens, launching a series of drop assaults against the secondary reactors that power the Titan's arsenal. Metraen's forces succeed in neutralising the Titan's defences and the White Scars swarm the lower levels. Though Voldorius ultimately escapes, his followers are exterminated almost to the last man. Though Kor'sarro Khan's hunt must continue, Zoran has been reclaimed for the Emperor, and the reclamation of a battered, but reparable, Imperator Titan is no small prize. Metraen brings the Titan hulk back to Baal, from where it is sent to Mars, Dante doubtless hoping that the gift will smooth over the Adeptus Mechanicus' quarrels with his Chapter.

877.M41 The Mel'yanneth Skywar.

Captain Metraen is charged with destruction of the Eldar Raiders operating from a fortress hidden in the poisonous atmosphere of the gas giant Mel'yanneth. Harnessing the Chapter's entire fleet of Stormraven and Thunderhawk Gunships, Metraen initiates an unprecedented airborne assault. Stormravens jink though the blaze of anti-aircraft fire to disgorge Assault Squads and Terminators directly onto the floating fortress' docking platforms, securing landing zones for Land Raiders and Predators to arrive via Thunderhawk Transporters.

As the battle rages through the fortress' hangars and service shafts, the overwhelming firepower and determination of the Blood Angels is little abated by the Eldar's arcane traps and dishonourable defensive systems. Realising the hopelessness of their situation, the aliens abandon their fortress, although not before sabotaging its gravity nullifiers.

Metraen is forced to retreat as the fortress' remains are inexorably sucked into Mel'yanneth's hungry maw. Only the incredible skill of the Blood Angels gunship pilots, who fearlessly plunge their craft into the deepening gravity well to rescue their Battle-Brothers, prevents the victory becoming a crushing defeat.

901.M41 The Battle of Stonehaven.

Commander Dante leads the Stormraven drop assault that finally breaks Waaagh! Bludcrumpa's decade-long siege on forge world Ironhelm.

911.M41 The Vengeance of the Blood Angels.

Justicar Parsival of the Grey Knights brings word to Baal that the hated Bloodthirster Ka'Bandha is once more at large in the mortal realm. Sepharan, leader of the Sanguinary Guard, seeks and receives Dante's permission for the Sanguinary Guard to join the coming battle. United in purpose, the Grey Knights and Sanguinary Guard storm the gates of Ka'Bandha's unholy fortress, laying waste to the Greater Daemon and his army in a single night of glorious battle.

918.M41 The Semmel Betrayal.

Blood Angels strike force *Breath of Hermes* comes under attack by Eldar on the ghost world of Semmel. Early dispatches from the battle indicate that the Blood Angels briefly held the upper hand, until an unknown party came to the Eldar's aid. The strike force is wiped out to the last Battle-Brother.

926.M41 The Worldengine.

The Blood Angels 2nd and 4th Companies are despatched to the Vidar Sector to assist against the threat of the Necron Worldengine. Following the sacrifice of the Astral Knights Chapter and the destruction of the Worldengine, it is Captain Donatos Aphael of the 2nd Company who proposes that a permanent shrine to the Astral Knights be raised upon the planet of Safehold. From that day forth, two Blood Angels of the 2nd Company are permanently assigned to stand guard over the memorial.

927.M41 The Battle for Antax.

Captain Aphael liberates the forge world of Antax from Waaagh! Gutstompa.

930.M41 Day of the Swordwind.

Only the stalwart actions of the Blood Angels 3rd Company preserve Explorator Station Ghosa Prime from the unprovoked fury of the Biel-Tann Eldar.

941.M41 The Second Battle for Armageddon.

Waaagh! Ghazghkull descends upon the hive world of Armageddon. The Blood Angels are one of three Space Marine Chapters to respond. Such is Commander Dante's reputation that Tu'shan of the Salamanders and Marneus Calgar of the Ultramarines cede overall command to him.

Fighting is fierce in and around the hive cities, with the determination of the defenders matched only by the unremitting battle-lust of the Orks. The Blood Angels bear the brunt of the close-quarter fighting, chiefly because only the overcharged engines of their Lucifer-class Rhinos can hope to keep pace with the roaming convoys of Ork Trukks and Battlewagons.

The tactical manoeuvrability of the Blood Angels proves to be crucial in the later stages of the campaign. The 3rd Company, under the command of the newly promoted Captain Erasmus Tycho, forms the heart of an armoured spearhead that cripples the chief Ork supply lines, leaving the Waaagh!'s Mekboyz without the necessary gubbins and gears to keep the massive Skullhammas and Stompas fully operational. With its 'eavy guns thus neutralised, the Waaagh! is finally broken before the towering walls of Tartarus Hive, where Dante and Tu'shan famously fight side by side against Ghazghkull's bodyguard.

955.M41 The Gehenna Campaign.

Commander Dante and the 3rd Company battle against the Necron Legions of the Silent King amidst the dusty wastes of Gehenna. For three weeks, neither side can seize the upper hand, with Dante's tactical brilliance stretched to its limits in countering the time-space manipulations of the Silent King. The stalemate is broken only when a Tyranid splinter fleet enters orbit, forcing the two armies to break off hostilities and fight the common foe. The impromptu alliance proves to be the Tyranids' undoing. Following the final battle at Devil's Crag, Dante and the Silent King go their separate ways, both forces now too battleworn to guarantee victory over the other, and, at least for the Blood Angels, the idea of turning on those they had so recently fought alongside, a rather distasteful one.

965.M41 The Temptation of Mephiston.

Daemon Prince M'kar the Reborn traps Chief Librarian Mephiston in the crystal caverns of Solon V. He attempts to lure Mephiston onto the path of the Renegade, accusing him of being firmly on the path to daemonhood. Rejecting M'kar's dastardly deceptions, Mephiston throttles the life out of his captor, but not before a sinister seed of doubt worms its way into his heroic heart.

990.M41 The Vaults of Pandrax.

In his search for a cure to the Flaw, Brother Corbulo finds the ancient archeotech repositories of Pandrax III in the hands of the Alaitoc Eldar. Three companies of Blood Angels, including the famous 1st Company Terminators, are assigned to seize the vaults from alien interlopers. Fierce battle soon rages through the tech-vaults and catacombs. The Blood Angels are ultimately victorious, but the Farseer commanding the Eldar efforts sacrifices himself to destroy the very records Corbulo seeks. The search must begin again.

991.M41 The Stromark Civil War.

Political rivalry in the Stromark system leads to civil war between the two manufactorum worlds. The escalating conflict quickly halts much-needed weapons supplies to the Imperium, a situation that cannot be allowed to continue. So it is that the Angels Encarmine and the Flesh Tearers Chapters are dispatched to the Stromark system with orders to end the conflict by any means necessary.

The fighting on Stromark Prime ceases first. Indeed, the first engagement by the Flesh Tearers Chapter is also the last on that planet. The stories of unstoppable Space Marines hacking a bloody path through thousands upon thousands of Stromarkian warriors quickly terrify the planet's populace into subservience.

Stromark Secundus takes a little longer to fall, the Angels Encarmine being a little less direct in their methods than the Flesh Tearers, and several hours of hard fighting follow. Nonetheless, when five of the Chapter's Furioso Dreadnoughts smash into the military headquarters and tear the High Command limb from limb, the surviving officers wisely choose to end the conflict.

In the wake of the slaughter, officials from the Adeptus Munitorum estimate that the damage caused by the civil war, and the rather larger amount of damage caused by the Space Marine assault, will take centuries to repair.

992.M41 The Hives of Hollonan.

In response to a request for assistance, Chief Librarian Mephiston leads strike force *Sanguinatus* to the hive world of Hollonan. What at first appears to be a mere, if substantial, rebellion, is swiftly revealed to be a deep-rooted Genestealer infestation. Mephiston's strike force purges the alien parasites from the hives of Hollonan, but it is too late – even as the last Genestealer brood is purged, ships from a Hive Fleet Kraken splinter fleet arrives in the Hollonan system. Recognising that his force cannot repel a Tyranid onslaught of that magnitude, Mephiston takes command of Hollonan and sends a request for assistance to distant Baal and to Corinal – the nearby Chapter planet of the Angels Vermillion.

The ensuing battles in the depths of Hollonan strain even the battle-lust of the Blood Angels. The first Tyranid strike neutralises the planetary defence batteries and automated sentry guns. The second annihilates the chain of antiquated, but vital, fusion accumulators that provide Hollonan with much of its power. What results is a terrifying battle for survival in the guts of Hollonan's underhive, with Mephiston's Blood Angels stretched to the limit as they rally the planet's defence force against the endless hordes of Termagants, Raveners and Carnifexes.

Only where Mephiston fights do the forces of humanity hold. In those two dreadful weeks, the Librarian proves his might time and time again, never once sleeping or taking rest, always carrying the fight to the alien invaders, though even his Battle-Brothers are weary to the bone. His deeds are legend. At the Chapel of the Emperor's Repose, Mephiston tears a Carnifex to ichor-stained shreds with his bare hands. He holds the ruined entrance to the filtration plant for six hours without aid. And in the final hours of that terrible invasion, he cleaves his way alone through the Hive Mind brood that spearheads the assault, laying low the vile Hive Tyrant and all his foul guardians before he is himself struck down by a Trygon.

Mephiston's fall, which could have so easily robbed the heart from the defenders, instead drives them to redoubled effort. Such is the battle-spirit roused in those weary Blood Angels and warriors of Hollonan that they survive long enough for the desperately awaited reinforcements to arrive.

Like the avenging angels they are, fresh companies of Blood Angels and Angels Vermillion scream from the skies in Drop Pods and Stormraven Gunships – but they are not alone. The Eldar of Ulthwé, led by the ancient Farseer Eldrad Ulthran, make planetfall alongside the Space Marines, fighting beside humanity for their own enigmatic reasons. The Tyranids are crushed between the three descending armies, this splinter of Hive Fleet Kraken is scoured from existence. Eldrad Ulthran remains just long enough to see Mephiston recovered from the rubble, grievously wounded but alive – a second resurrection that serves only to increase Mephiston's legend through his Chapter.

994.M41 The Blackfang Crusade.

Judging that the Ork strongholds in the Blackfang system have defied the Imperium for too long, Dante mobilises the entire Chapter in a year-long campaign that not only drives the Orks from the twelve worlds of Blackfang, but also from two neighbouring systems.

995.M41 Beheading the Serpent.

Tycho's 3rd Company is one of many Space Marine strike forces that responds to the threat of Hive Fleet Jormungandr. Though Tycho leads his Battle-Brothers to several crucial victories, so reckless are his tactics that the Sanguinary Priests begin to fear for his sanity.

996.M41 Vengeance for Semmel.

Dante learns the location of the Eldar who slew so many of his Battle-Brothers on Semmel and orders the Sanguinary Guard to enact vengeance. The strike force catches up with its quarry in the arid badlands of Zoros. In the resulting aerial battle, Sanguinary Guardians duel with Eldar Jetbikes and Swooping Hawk Aspect Warriors, but finally emerge victorious. Alas, the identity of the Semmel Betrayer cannot be discovered, so the Blood Angels' ultimate vengeance remains elusive.

998.M41 The Third Battle for Armageddon.

Ghazghkull returns to the arid world at the head of another, vaster Waaagh! Over two dozen Space Marine Chapters respond this time, which is fortunate as the Blood Angels are forced to deploy much of their strength against the growing threat of Hive Fleet Leviathan. Nonetheless, honour demands that the Chapter provides assistance to beleaguered Armageddon and Dante sends his 3rd Company and a generous complement of support units. In the course of the campaign. Captain Tycho finally succumbs to the Black Rage and dies a valiant death on the outer walls of Hive Tempestora. Command of the 3rd Company passes to Galan Machiavi.

999.M41 The Darkest Hour.

The Blood Angels are tested as never before. A tendril of Hive Fleet Leviathan is judged to be on a direct course for Baal. Worse, the dread Ka'Bandha returns from the darkness of the Warp with a Daemon army at his command, his first blow striking against Ammonai, outermost planet of the Baal system.

Faced with a terrible war on at least two fronts, Dante makes swift preparation, uniting many Imperial and non-human worlds under the banner of survival. Even some former foes can be counted in Dante's alliance, though whether or not they can be entirely trusted is another matter. Knowing even these forces are not enough to repel both Daemons and Tyranids, Dante recalls the 3rd Company from Armageddon and sends requests for aid to the Blood Angels' successors. The Flesh Tearers are the first to respond, dispatching their full fighting strength without hesitation, and ultimately all but the Lamentors lend aid to their primogenitor. Even the Knights of Blood, declared Renegade many centuries earlier, heed the call – though they are careful never to take the field alongside the other Chapters.

So is the stage set for the defence of Baal itself – perhaps the final battle of the Scions of Sanguinius...

BLOOD ON KHARTAS

The Blood Angels Strike Cruiser *Baal's Fist* was returning from campaign in the Wotan Sector when the distress call was received. The planet Khartas was perhaps not the most resplendent jewel in the Imperium's crown – the Wars of Ruination a century earlier had left much of the northern hemisphere shattered and lifeless – but it was nonetheless too important a contributor to the Imperium's war materiel to leave at the mercy of pirates. Thus Captain Abel Zorael ordered the *Baal's Fist* onto a new course in order to bring what aid he could to Khartas.

Through luck or judgement, *Baal's Fist* emerged from Warp space practically on top of the pirate fleet, its precise broadsides obliterating several escort craft before engaging the pirate flagship *Slaughterer's Laughter*. The pirate cruiser fared little better than its companions – its weapons batteries were knocked out in the Blood Angels' first salvo, whilst the second all but crippled its engines.

Bereft of all but the most feeble motive power, *Slaughterer's Laughter* was quickly captured by Khartas' gravity well. The pirate vessel tumbled incandescently through the atmosphere, finally slamming to a halt amid the ruins of one of Khartas' northern cities. Not wanting any surviving pirates to go to ground and thus return to bedevil Khartas further, Captain Zorael led three squads of Blood Angels to the planet's surface. Alas, what seemed to be a simple seek-and-destroy mission would swiftly grow more serious.

The *Slaughterer's Laughter*'s Warp drive had been heavily damaged but not entirely destroyed. Though the colossal engines would never again move a vessel through the vagaries of Warp space, some fluke of impact with the planet's surface brought them flickering to erratic and unstable life. Uncontrolled, the cascading energies tore a rent in the physical world, creating a pervasive portal to the dread daemonlands of the Realm of Chaos. Zorael had been correct in assuming that many of the *Slaughterer's Laughter*'s crew had survived the crash, but none of them long survived the ebon blades of the daemon-host that burst through into the mortal world.

Captain Zorael's first hint that something was awry came swiftly afterward. An otherworldly storm sprang up as his three Stormraven Gunships made their final approach to the crash site. The craft were buffeted by swirling winds and pounded by crimson lightning. One by one, thrusters screaming as they fought the unnatural weather, the Stormravens fell from the sky. The surviving Blood Angels pried their way out of their stricken transports to find themselves scattered and stranded in a ruined city crawling with cackling Bloodletters. Bellowing to be heard above the swirling storm, Zorael ordered his Battle-Brothers to regroup within the comparative shelter of nearby ruins. As he did so, an ear-splitting howl went up all around as the Bloodletters noticed the fresh prey in their midst. Boltguns roared as the Blood Angels fought their way to shelter, the raucous din momentarily drowning out the daemonic cries, but then a monstrous Bloodthirster dove out of the skies above, bellowing a challenge whose furious tones were clear even over the boltguns' wrath.

Zorael's Last Stand

No mere Bloodthirster was this, but Ka'Bandha, first amongst Khorne's servants and heir to power and stature easily thrice that of others of his kind. In times past it was he who had crippled Sanguinius amongst the killing fields of Signus Prime, he who had singlehandedly put the nine worlds of Koros to sword. In the final days of the Horus Heresy, it was Ka'Bandha who had duelled Sanguinius before the Emperor's palace. The Primarch had bested the Greater Daemon that day, breaking the monster's back and casting him lifeless to the ground, yet Ka'Bandha was of daemonkind and not even the blows of great Sanguinius could forever stay his wrath. In all the ages of the galaxy, no other creature had taken more skulls for the Blood God or done so more joyfully. Ka'Bandha was death personified, yet Zorael did not flinch. Shouting his own challenge, the Captain charged into the fray.

Two, perhaps three strikes did Zorael land upon his bellowing adversary, but no more. The Bloodthirster's axe, unholy runes glowing crimson, came down in one massive blow. Zorael brought his own blade up to counter the strike, but Ka'Bandha's Warp-forged axe was not to be thwarted by any mortal weapon, be it an honoured relic of the Blood Angels or no. Down drove the Bloodthirster's axe, shattering the weapon that sought to prevent its passage, cleaving through Zorael's armour and driving deep into his flesh. As the mortally wounded Captain sank defenceless to his knees, Ka'Bandha stooped low over the fallen corpse. The Bloodthirster reached out a betaloned hand and, with contemptuous ease, tore Zorael's head from his shoulders. Roaring with victory, Ka'Bandha brandished his trophy high for a moment before lowering it into his fanged maw to crunch the skull with his monstrous teeth.

With the fall of their Captain, dismay threatened to steal over the surviving Blood Angels. If the mightiest of their number had done little save to slow the rampaging Bloodthirster, what hope did they have? Heavy weaponry could perhaps be brought to bear against the brute, but already the Devastators' positions were overrun, the survivors engaged in brutal hand-to-hand combat atop a rampart formed from their slain Battle-Brothers. Rescue was impossible, for the same daemonstorm that had grounded Zorael's Stormravens would surely spell the doom of other craft. In such dire circumstances, lesser warriors would perhaps have ceded all hope, yet these were Space Marines of the Blood Angels Chapter, the sons of honoured Sanguinius. Their forebears had fought beside the Emperor in the very blackest of days, and that memory was not theirs to dishonour. In an instant, the shadow passed from the hearts of the beset Battle-Brothers, replaced by fresh determination. Boltguns roared once again to scythe down fresh waves of Bloodletters, and those Blood Angels already trapped in melee unleashed their own rage, summoning a battle-fury that even the blood-slicked Daemons of the Warp could not endure.

Alas, this newfound defiance could not alter the course of the battle, only prolong it. The Blood Angels were few, whilst the Daemons were beyond counting and ever-reinforced through the Warp-portal fed by the *Slaughterer's Laughter*'s engines. Now Ka'Bandha, hungry to claim more skulls, sprang into the fray once more. Taking wing, the Bloodthirster fixed his baleful attentions upon the site of greatest resistance – a handful of Blood Angels whose defensive position amongst the tumbled ruin of an Imperial shrine had, as yet, thwarted all onslaughts. Ka'Bandha rode his mighty wings ever higher through the daemonstorm, seeking to plunge down upon his prey. Yet, at the apex of the Bloodthirster's ascent, everything changed. A golden figure hurtled out of the heavens like a meteor, slamming into Ka'Bandha with bone-crushing force. The Sanguinor, legendary protector of the Blood Angels, had arrived.

The Angel and the Daemon
So furious was the Sanguinor's impact that not even Ka'Bandha's mighty wings could keep the Bloodthirster skyborne. Angel and Daemon tumbled from the air and smote the ground with incredible force, their impact furrowing a fresh scar across the ruins. No sooner had the adversaries come to rest than their battle began in earnest. At first glance it seemed a clash scarcely less uneven than the Bloodthirster's previous duel. Ka'Bandha had taken the brunt of the skyfall, his wings twisted and broken by the impact – fresh harms to join those wounds inflicted by Zorael. But Ka'Bandha was still a dread opponent, the most deadly of a savage breed. Beside the musculous might of Ka'Bandha, the Sanguinor seemed insignificant, a candle-flame threatened to be snuffed out by a tide of blood and darkness. Yet still the winged warrior stood his ground, his golden armour shining bright.

The Sanguinor was far swifter than his foe, gracefully evading each swing of Ka'Bandha's rune axe, almost as if he knew every feat of which the beast was capable. For every blow thus evaded, the Sanguinor struck out in return, his blade biting deep into Ka'Bandha's unholy flesh, the Daemon's dark ichor bubbling and steaming upon contact with the open air. Bellowing in rage and pain, Ka'Bandha lashed out with his barbed whip. The coils closed around the Sanguinor's throat, finally pinioning the golden angel long enough for the Bloodthirster to land a telling strike of his own, a thunderous axe-blow that tore the Sanguinor free of the lash, while the force of impact caused the axe to shatter much as Zorael's sword had before. Red-hot shards of the sundered axe flashing all around, the Sanguinor was sent

crashing through a ferrocrete wall. Yet in moments the golden angel was on his feet once more, his armour smouldering where the hell-forged axe had struck, but otherwise seemingly unharmed.

Again Ka'Bandha's whip struck out, but this time the Sanguinor caught the tip in his gauntleted hand. Though he was driven to his knees by the impact, the Sanguinor struck out with his blade, severing the lash near to its haft. Riding the momentum of the blow, the Sanguinor threw himself forward, plunging his sword into Ka'Bandha's chest with all the might at his command. Yet even this did not slay the Daemon, who merely roared anew and sent the Sanguinor sprawling with a contemptuous backhanded blow.

The Final Strike
The combatants were now weaponless, the Bloodthirster's axe in ruins and the Sanguinor's blade embedded in the Daemon's flesh. Both were worn and weary, the Sanguinor's light perhaps dimmer than it had been, Ka'Bandha's massive frame oozing daemonblood from scores of wounds. In a final desperate gambit, the Sanguinor triggered his jump pack, hurling himself at the Bloodthirster once more, one hand closing around the hilt of his abandoned sword, the other finding purchase on the creature's brazen armour. Skywards did the Sanguinor take himself and his opponent, pushing his tortured jump pack to the limit, enduring Ka'Bandha's bludgeoning blows as best he could. Higher and higher they flew, through the lightning and rage of the daemonstorm to where the air began to thin in gravity's weakening grasp. Only then did the Sanguinor release his hold upon the Daemon's armour. Closing both hands around the hilt of his sword, the Sanguinor planted both feet firmly upon Ka'Bandha's chest and pulled the ancient blade free. No longer held aloft by the efforts of the Sanguinor's jump pack, and his own wings rendered broken and useless from wounds, Ka'Bandha plummeted from the heavens, speeding faster and faster as Khartas' gravity grasped him ever tighter. It is said that the sound of Ka'Bandha's final craterous impact could be heard in every corner of the planet. His body broken beyond repair, Ka'bandha's spirit fled back to grovel before his unholy master's throne of skulls.

Ka'Bandha's blood was not the last that the Sanguinor's blade tasted that day. Swooping low over the battlefield, he cast the tide of Bloodletters from his Battle-Brothers. A small measure of respite gained, the Sanguinor roused the surviving Blood Angels to one last effort, his clarion tones redoubling their strength, his example reforging their purpose. Thus ennobled, the Blood Angels attacked once more, fighting their way to the wreckage of the downed cruiser whose misfiring Warp drive had wrought their woes. A few well-placed meltabombs later, and the Warp drive, and the portal it had spawned, were silenced forever.

The daemonstorm had abated with Ka'Bandha's death, and soon gunships descended from *Baal's Fist* to retrieve the survivors and the slain. Of the thirty Space Marines who had made planetfall on Khartas, only six would fight again. As for the Sanguinor? He vanished in the final moments of the battle, leaving the field as mysteriously as he had arrived. None amongst the survivors believed him to have been slain, though they had no tangible proof either way. It was to be many years before he was sighted again...

BATTLE FOR ANTAX

Of all the planets in the Vidar sector that could have fallen into the hands of Waaagh! Gutstompa's Meks, Antax was about the worst. As one of the sector's principal forge worlds, Antax was an Ork Loota's wildest dream, packed from archeotech vault to orbital station with all manner of arcane technology and, of course, thousands of really big guns. Even accounting for the fact that a good proportion of the stolen weaponry would doubtless be destroyed through the traditional Mek method of wiring different things together in order to see what would happen, Antax's fall was a disaster. The supply lines for hundreds of Imperial Guard regiments and a dozen Space Marine Chapters were now cut, and those same weapons and tanks were certain to be used against their rightful recipients. So it was that, though his Battle-Brothers were weary from their part in the battle against the Necron Worldengine, Captain Aphael of the Blood Angels turned his strike force aside from its homeward path, and set course for beleaguered Antax.

As the Battle Barge *Blade of Vengeance* and its Strike Cruiser escort arrived in orbit around the fallen forge world, the scale of the battle quickly became apparent. The planet's outer atmosphere was choked with the blackened and twisted remains of countless space vessels, some doubtless the broken fragments of Antax's defence fleet, others unmistakably the burnt-out hulks of Ork craft. The wrecked greenskin vessels vastly outnumbered those of the Adeptus Mechanicus fleet – evidently Antax's defenders had given a good account of themselves before they were overwhelmed. The only surviving Ork vessels appeared now to have landed, or possibly crashed, on the planet's surface, a short distance from the towering pinnacles of the Mechanicus Prime Forge – an obvious target and one too good to miss. In response to Aphael's commands, the *Blade of Vengeance* swung into a new orbit and unleashed a blistering bombardment that tore the grounded Ork vessels apart. The skies now belonged to the Blood Angels.

The Assault Begins

Scarcely had the Battle Barge's guns fallen silent than Aphael assembled his senior sergeants and composed a plan of attack. No communications had been received to indicate the presence of Adeptus Mechanicus survivors on Antax, yet Exterminatus could be considered only as a last resort, so great were the technological treasures housed within the forge world's vaults. Thus the Orks would have to be rooted out from the planet, though they numbered in their tens of thousands and the Blood Angels were but a few hundred. Fortunately, the Waaagh! had splintered. Scores upon scores of warbands roamed Antax's surface, searching for lootable technology – only around the Prime Forge did a sizable horde remain. Against the smaller warbands, Aphael dispatched half his Battle-Brothers, organised into five- and ten-man task forces and supported by the strike force's Stormraven Gunships. Yet the real fight would occur in the shadow of the Prime Forge. The heavy Ork presence there suggested that either some of Antax's defenders still held out in that area, or that some particularly precious salvage could there be found. Either way, further orbital bombardments could not be risked – the Battle for Antax would now have to be fought eye-to-eye with the Orks.

Brooking no delay, Aphael and his remaining warriors began their Drop Pod assault, slamming into the Ork defences like thunderbolts from an angry sky. The orbital bombardment had ensured that the Orks were not taken unawares by the Blood Angels onslaught, but nor had they had the chance to fully prepare for the descending assault. Only a handful of minutes had separated the last echoing barrage and the arrival of the first Drop Pod. Gutstompa had not even begun to beat some much needed order into his lads when the first hatches slammed open and the volleys of boltgun fire began to cut the greenskins down. Taking advantage of the confusion, the Blood Angels surged forwards across the broken flagstones and tumbled statues that surrounded the Prime Forge, boltguns roaring as they drove the Orks before them. Hundreds of Orks fell to the fury of the Blood Angels in those first few moments of the battle, but now Gutstompa launched his counter-attack. With a throaty rumble that made the battlefield tremble, the gates of the Prime Forge swung open and a tide of greenskins poured into the fray. Gutstompa himself led this fresh horde from the command deck of his Kustom Battlewagon. Around the tank were the Warboss' Mega-armoured bodyguards, huge brutes that strode unflinching into the hail of bolter fire.

It was then that Aphael's plan threatened to come undone. Even as the fresh wave of Orks charged forwards, Squad Atreon succumbed to the Red Thirst. Overcome by bloodlust, the Devastators cast down their heavy bolters and charged headlong at the Orks, only to be swallowed by the green tide. Aphael cursed silently to himself as his brothers fell – the loss of Squad Atreon's firepower could easily sway the course of battle. Worse, the Captain could feel the Red Thirst calling to him also, its taste thick in his throat, the battlelust challenging his every action of restraint. Forcing back the demon in his blood through sheer force of will, Aphael shifted his forces to meet the new threat. Moment by moment, more Battle-Brothers fell. Even though each claimed a score of Orks before succumbing to death or injury, the greenskins were many and the Space Marines few. The piles of dead and wounded grew on both sides, but still Gutstompa and his bodyguard came on, set to crush the upstart Blood Angels Captain who stood in his path. Fortunately, Aphael had one final weapon to call upon.

The Vengeance of the Lost

On the eve of the struggle with the Worldengine, near a dozen Battle-Brothers had succumbed to the Black Rage, their rational minds subsumed by the horrors of Sanguinius' fall. In any other engagement, these lost Blood Angels would have formed the strike force's Death Company, spearheading Aphael's assaults. Yet the Blood Angels' part in the Worldengine battle had been entirely spaceborne, and there had been no opportunity for the Death Company to earn glorious oblivion. Therefore, Aphael had ordered those afflicted to be placed in stasis, so that their sacrifice could come at an hour when it was needed – that hour had now come. Even before Aphael had left the Battle Barge, the Sanguinary Priests cracked the seals of the stasis chambers and performed the rites of renewal. The awoken Death Company were given over to the command of the strike force Chaplains and taken aboard the Stormraven *Red Glory*.

They would not fight alone. As the Sanguinary Priests laboured to awaken the cursed living, in the bowels of the *Blade of Vengeance*, the Techmarines set their minds to the revival of one long dead – the mighty Death Company Dreadnought, Moriar the Chosen. Whispering the hymnals of awakening and invigoration, the Techmarines drove the fog of slumber from Moriar's crazed mind, girded his adamantium frame with weapons of war and the sacraments of sacrifice. When the *Red Glory* left the docking hangar, it did so with a full complement of Death Company aboard, and with Moriar securely grappled beneath its wings.

The *Red Glory* struck without warning, speeding from the heavens like an angel of vengeance. On the gunship's first pass, twin missiles shot out from under its wings, contrails twisting lazily in the sky as they slammed into Gutstompa's Battlewagon and blew it to flaming fragments, sending the furious Warboss flying. On the second pass, the Stormraven Gunship turned the fury of its hurricane bolters and assault cannons onto the greenskin horde, mowing down Orks left and right, before spurring out of range of retaliatory fire. On its third pass, the *Red Glory*'s hatches burst open in mid-air, Moriar's grapples were released, and the Death Company hurled themselves into the fray.

The Death Company were outnumbered, encircled and had no hope of survival, but hope and survival were no longer concepts they understood. They hacked at the Orks with chainsword and combat blade, and when those weapons were lost or ruined, the Death Company tore at the greenskins with their gauntleted hands and bared teeth. Wounds that should have been fatal seemed only to slow the Death Company, and then never for long. Never before

had these Orks fought a foe so reckless and furious, and they trampled one another in their attempts to escape the onset of the frenzied warriors whose armour was slick with the blood of the slain. For a moment, Gutstompa's Mega-armoured bodyguard managed to halt the Death Company's advance – not even the Blood Angels' rage-fuelled strength could penetrate the Nobs' armoured hides – but then Moriar's adamantium bulk charged forward, smashing the Nobs aside with mighty blows.

Victory Born of Fury

As the Death Company tore the heart out of Gutstompa's counter-attack, the remaining Blood Angels redoubled their efforts. With a roar, Aphael finally succumbed to the rising battlelust within his soul. Now was not the time for measured strategy, but for unbound rage. As the Captain charged forward over the blood-slicked ground, other Blood Angels took up his battlecry. Rising up from their defensive positions, the Sons of Sanguinius charged headlong at the beset Orks, their inner rage now become a thing of strength, not weakness. Seeing his dreams of loot and conquest about to be drowned in gore, Gutstompa bellowed for reinforcements, but Aphael's other task forces had done their work well. Those Ork warbands not already slain were fighting for their lives elsewhere, and the only Boyz Gutstompa could call upon were even now fighting and dying around him. By the time the Warboss fell, torn apart by Moriar himself, the heart had long since gone out his Waaagh!

A scant hour later, with the Red Thirst slaked and the Orks all but obliterated, the hunt for survivors began. Antax belonged to the Imperium once more.

THE ANGELIC HOST

This section of the book details the forces used by the Blood Angels – their weapons, their units, and some famous special characters that you can choose, such as Commander Dante. Each entry describes the unit and gives the specific rules you will need to use them in your games. As such, the army list given later refers to the page numbers of these entries, so you can easily check back as you pick a force.

The Angelic Host section is sub-divided into two parts. The first part describes all of the troops and vehicles fielded by the Blood Angels, including the special characters, while the second part details the Blood Angels armoury of weapons and equipment.

Equipment

The army list at the back of the book shows all the standard and optional wargear available to a particular model. You will find that some items of equipment are unique to particular characters or units, while others are used by more than one unit. When an item is unique, it is detailed in the relevant entry for its owner, and where an item is not unique, it is detailed in the wargear section.

A good example is the Axe Mortalis, a potent weapon wielded by Commander Dante. As such, its rules are detailed in Dante's entry. Dante also carries an infernus pistol. This weapon is also carried by other Blood Angels, and so its rules are to be found in the wargear section.

BLOOD ANGELS SPECIAL RULES

The models in the Blood Angels army use a number of special rules that are common to more than one unit, as specified in the individual entries that follow. Details of those shared rules are given here. If a special rule is not explained on this page or in the relevant entry, it can be found within the main Warhammer 40,000 rulebook.

And They Shall Know No Fear

Blood Angels automatically pass tests to regroup, and can take such tests even if the squad has been reduced to less than half strength by casualties, though all other criteria apply. Usually troops that regroup cannot move normally and always count as moving whether they do or not, but these restrictions do not apply to models subject to this special rule.

If Blood Angels are caught by a sweeping advance, they are not destroyed and will instead continue to fight normally. If this happens then the unit is subject to the No Retreat! rule in this round of close combat and might therefore suffer additional casualties.

Units which include Servitors are still subject to this rule, providing that the unit contains at least one Blood Angels Space Marine model.

Combat Squads

Units with this special rule that include ten squad members have the option of breaking down into two five-man units, called combat squads. For example, a ten-man Sternguard Veterans squad can fight as a ten-man unit or break down into two five-man combat squads.

The decision to split the unit into combat squads, as well as which models go into each combat squad, must be made when the unit is deployed. Both combat squads can be deployed in separate locations. The one exception to this is a unit that arrives by Drop Pod – the player can choose to split such a unit into combat squads when it disembarks.

If you decide to split a unit into combat squads, then each combat squad is treated as a separate unit for all game purposes from that point.

Descent of Angels

Inclined to mastery of the heavens by temperament and lineage, the Blood Angels long ago refined the art of airborne assault via jump pack. Due to endless hours of battledrill, a Blood Angels jump pack assault can make planetfall with a precision and coordination at which other armies can only marvel and fear.

A Blood Angels unit with this special rule can re-roll failed reserve rolls if arriving by Deep Strike. Also, due to the precision of their descent, it scatter D6" less (normally D6" rather than 2D6").

Other units in the Blood Angels army that can arrive by Deep Strike do so using the normal rules.

The Red Thirst

Though every Blood Angel tries to suppress it, the Red Thirst ever lurks on the border of his soul, threatening at any moment to tip him into unstoppable fury. Sometimes the lure is too strong – otherwise sane Battle-Brothers find themselves temporarily gripped by the insane bloodlust of the Red Thirst, and all hopes of an ordered battle plan have to be abandoned.

After forces have been deployed, but before any scout moves are taken and the first turn begins, roll a D6 for each unit in your army that has this special rule (including units you have left in reserve). On a score of a 1, one or more members of the squad have succumbed to the Red Thirst and the entire squad is treated as having the Furious Charge and Fearless special rules instead of the And They Shall Know No Fear special rule for the duration of the game.

TACTICAL SQUADS

To be a member of a Tactical squad is to have proven yourself beyond all doubt in every aspect of war. Only when a Blood Angel has proven his worth in the Assault and Devastator Squads will he earn his place amongst the Chapter's Tactical Marines. For a Blood Angel in particular, to aspire to service in a Tactical Squad is to marshal the necessary control over the rage within; to act according to the situation at hand, rather than heed the chained beast in his soul. Not all Blood Angels earn such a position. For some, the lure of blood-drenched assault is too strong – such Battle-Brothers serve forever in the Chapter's Assault Squads until death or the Black Rage takes them. Other Blood Angels simply do not have the mental dexterity to switch between assault, close support and fire support roles as the situation requires. Only the very best Blood Angels serve in the Tactical Squads.

Most Tactical Marines carry a boltgun – the merciless weapon of death upon which the Imperium was founded. The squad's fearsome amount of anti-personnel firepower is inevitably complemented by a special weapon, such as a flamer or meltagun, as well as a heavy weapon of some kind. Missile launchers are most usually selected, though more specialised weapons, such as heavy bolters and lascannons, are also common. Each Blood Angel in a Tactical Squad is fully trained and capable with every weapon that their squad can be called upon to field. Therefore weaponry duties are not fixed, but rotated around the squad to ensure that the various firearms skills remain sharp.

As their name suggests, Tactical Squads are the most flexible and adaptable units present in a Blood Angels strike force. They can hold ground in a manner that Assault Squads cannot, and advance to new positions more swiftly than a Devastator Squad. As such, the Tactical Squad's role in any given battle will be defined more by circumstance than strict battle plan. The sergeant will be aware of his overall mission goals, but the method through which those goals are to be achieved is often left to his discretion, rather than enforced by the strike force commander.

Such is the experience wielded by the sergeants of Tactical Squads that their seniority and authority is second only to that of their Company Captain. It is not unusual for a senior sergeant to be given command over several other squads at the battle's onset, allowing the Captain to focus his strategic and tactical acumen on a particular area of the conflict rather than dissipating it across the battlefront. Should the Captain be slain or otherwise eliminated, command of the strike force automatically and seamlessly passes to the most senior Tactical Sergeant. Only a foolish enemy would think this to their advantage however – any shortfall in experience a sergeant has in comparison to his fallen Captain is more than made up for by the newfound determination to avenge his fallen commander.

	WS	BS	S	T	W	I	A	Ld	Sv
Space Marine	4	4	4	4	1	4	1	8	3+
Space Marine Sergeant	4	4	4	4	1	4	2	9	3+

UNIT TYPE: Infantry.

WARGEAR: Power armour, boltgun, bolt pistol, frag and krak grenades.

SPECIAL RULES: And They Shall Know No Fear, Combat Squads, The Red Thirst.

"Blood calls out to blood, so they say. Let us spill that of our enemies with all due haste, that we may hear its cry all the clearer."

– Sergeant Arcula, Blood Angels 3rd Company

ASSAULT SQUADS

Assault Squads form the core of the Blood Angels' close-quarter shock troops. Jump packs blazing, they roar across the battlefield on wings of flame, assailing the enemy where he least expects it, winning victory through valour, courage and battle-fury.

Most Blood Angels graduate to service in an Assault Squad once their training as a Scout is complete. Here, a Blood Angel's role and duties will mesh most closely with his innate skills and aptitudes. An Assault Squad's mission is to overwhelm the enemy at close quarters, so there are far fewer dangers in assigning a hot-headed young-blood here than to a more nuanced or tactically flexible assignment, such as with a Devastator or Tactical Squad. Furthermore, all Blood Angels have an innate affinity towards aerial combat. Though the mutation that produced Sanguinius' wings has never been repeated, the Primarch's heirs share a love of flight that is impossible for another to understand. To a Blood Angel a jump pack is therefore no simple machine or battlefield tool. It is an extension of their physical form, a manifestation of the spiritual bond between Primarch and scion, and a reminder that even in death his hand still guides the Chapter.

Whilst Assault Marines are incredibly common in a Blood Angels strike force, this should not be taken to indicate that Assault Squads are more prevalent here than in other Chapters. As with much of the Blood Angels' organisation, the provision and composition of Assault Squads is tied to the Codex Astartes, so the specified formula of two Assault Squads per Battle Company, plus one reserve Assault Company is still adhered to. However, given the Blood Angels' predilection for jump packs in general, and close assault in particular, there is rarely a shortage of Battle-Brothers with suitable training and temperament to fill Assault Squad rosters as casualties occur. So it is that Assault Squads are likely to remain at full strength, even though the rest of the strike force be woefully undermanned.

Having such a large number of mobile and skilled Assault Marines only broadens a Blood Angels' commander's tactical options. Should a full-blown linebreaker assault not be appropriate to the task at hand, he can turn his hand to subtler ploys such as outflanking pincer strikes, hit-and-run ambushes and even low altitude insertion via Thunderhawk and Stormraven Gunships.

As even a single Assault Squad is too dire a threat to ignore, a carefully coordinated onslaught by two or more squads can present a wealth of devastating tactical possibilities as the enemy shifts their defence perimeter to counter the oncoming jump troops. Only the most numerous of armies can hope to control every approach to every mission critical objective, and even they can accidentally open a vulnerable chink in their perimeter when redeploying. At that point, all it takes is a single mistake, and a sufficiently alert Assault

Squad Sergeant to completely alter the course of the battle. Thanks to the mobility provided by the jump pack, what begins as a feint can be swiftly reinforced with other squads, a probing sortie transformed in moments into a terrible and ruinous force of destruction.

	WS	BS	S	T	W	I	A	Ld	Sv
Space Marine	4	4	4	4	1	4	1	8	3+
Space Marine Sergeant	4	4	4	4	1	4	2	9	3+

UNIT TYPE: Jump Infantry.

WARGEAR: Power armour, bolt pistol, chainsword, frag and krak grenades, jump pack.

SPECIAL RULES: And They Shall Know No Fear, Combat Squads, Descent of Angels, The Red Thirst.

"When war is eternal, the blood of the foe is the only coin that can enrich a warrior, and the glory of victory holds the only hope of final redemption."

– Brother Zargo, Blood Angels 3rd Company

DEVASTATOR SQUADS

Devastator Squads are a crucial part of the Blood Angels battlefield strategy, providing long range support with the Chapter's most powerful man-portable weaponry. When the Tactical and Assault squads advance, they do so under a hail of supporting Devastator fire that cripples vehicles and scythes infantry from key positions and objectives. The exact battle plan for a Devastator Squad is therefore an incredibly fluid and shifting thing. The sergeant must have a keen eye for suitable vantage points for his squad to occupy as it advances, and have shrewd grasp of priorities – sometimes the most important target is the smallest, not the largest.

A Devastator squad commonly carries four heavy weapons, the exact nature of which varies from engagement to engagement, with anti-tank lascannons and multi-meltas exchanged for infantry-shredding heavy bolters and plasma cannons as the battle requires. Traditionally, a Devastator squad will tote a mix of weaponry, in order to more readily adapt to the battle's challenges, although some commanders prefer a homogenous weapons load-out, purposefully equipping their Devastator squads to compensate for shortfalls elsewhere in the strike force. Any Battle-Brothers not equipped with heavy weaponry carry boltguns, acting as spotters and providing covering fire, making the Devastator Squad, in essence, a heavy Tactical Squad that is just as capable of engaging the enemy at short range as it is at a distance.

As the Blood Angels tactical doctrine is one of continuous advance, they can ill-afford for their Devastator Squads to be left behind by the flow of battle. Accordingly, it is common for Blood Angels Devastator Squads to receive priority when transport vehicles are assigned. Land Raiders, having far superior armour to Rhino and Razorback transports, can travel far more freely and brave the hottest fire zones on a battlefield, thus ensuring that a Devastator Squad can get into a viable support position swiftly and safely.

In other Chapters, the Devastator squad is traditionally the first progression a Space Marine will make after completing his training in a Scout squad. This allows the promoted Battle Brother his first taste of a war as a full Space Marine, without exposing an untested warrior to the chaotic heart of a battle. By contrast, the Blood Angels Devastator squads are thick with veteran Battle-Brothers, warriors who can be counted upon to hold the impetuous and reckless side of their nature in check in order to provide the Chapter with much-needed fire support. Only the most experienced and strong-willed Blood Angels can resist the urge to charge into the fray when blood starts flowing. Nonetheless, even the steadiest Devastator sergeant can occasionally succumb to the lure of close combat. Should the enemy come too close, they might well find themselves beset at far closer quarters than they had imagined.

	WS	BS	S	T	W	I	A	Ld	Sv
Space Marine	4	4	4	4	1	4	1	8	3+
Space Marine Sergeant	4	4	4	4	1	4	2	9	3+

UNIT TYPE: Infantry.

WARGEAR: Power armour, boltgun, bolt pistol, frag and krak grenades, (the Sergeant also has a signum).

SPECIAL RULES: And They Shall Know No Fear, Combat Squads, The Red Thirst.

"Though I long for the heady joys of blade-to-blade combat as much as any of my Brothers, command of such overwhelming firepower offers a satisfaction all of its own."

– Sergeant Traviola, Blood Angels 2nd Company

VETERAN SQUADS

A Blood Angel who serves with distinction will one day be elevated to the hallowed ranks of the Chapter's 1st (or Veteran) Company. Members of the 1st Company are living exemplars to their Battle-Brothers, true masters of the many weapons a Space Marine can be called upon to employ.

Unlike other troops, Veterans are permitted to select their own weaponry, rather than have it thrust upon them by tradition or doctrine. As a result, the Blood Angels' preference for close-quarter battle can be seen as clearly in the disposition of its 1st Company as it can elsewhere in the Chapter. Whilst the 1st Company follows the Codex Astartes' guidance that its squads be split into assault Veterans, known as Vanguard Squads, and Tactical Veterans, known as Sternguard Squads, the Chapter's Sternguard Squads are always outnumbered by Vanguards.

	WS	BS	S	T	W	I	A	Ld	Sv
Veteran	4	4	4	4	1	4	2	9	3+
Space Marine Sergeant	4	4	4	4	1	4	2	9	3+

UNIT TYPE: Infantry.

WARGEAR:
Vanguard Veteran Squad:
Power armour, bolt pistol, chainsword (the Sergeant has a power sword instead), frag and krak grenades.

Sternguard Veteran Squad:
Power armour, boltgun, bolt pistol, frag and krak grenades.

Special Issue Ammunition: Each time a Sternguard Veteran squad fires, the controlling player chooses which type of ammunition is being used. Each special ammunition type replaces the boltgun profile (including boltguns that are part of a combi-weapon) with the one shown here. All models in the squad must use the same ammunition type during that Shooting phase.

Dragonfire Bolts: These hollow shells explode with a gout of superheated gas that makes a mockery of cover.

Range	Strength	AP	Type
24"	4	5	Rapid Fire, Ignores Cover*

*Cover saves cannot be taken against dragonfire bolts.

Vengeance Rounds: These use unstable flux technology and are incredibly effective against armoured targets.

Range	Strength	AP	Type
18"	4	3	Rapid Fire, Gets Hot!

Kraken Bolts: The adamantine core and improved propellant of these bolts can penetrate the thickest hide.

Range	Strength	AP	Type
30"	4	4	Rapid Fire

Hellfire Rounds: Each hellfire round replaces the bolt's explosive charge with a chamber of voracious acid.

Range	Strength	AP	Type
24"	X	5	Rapid fire, Poisoned (2+)*

*Against targets with a Toughness value, hits from hellfire rounds will always wound on a roll of 2+.

SPECIAL RULES:
All Veterans:
And They Shall Know No Fear, Combat Squads, The Red Thirst.

Vanguard Veteran Squad only:
Heroic Intervention: Vanguard Veterans are famed for arriving at a time and place where their onslaught can make the most difference to a battle. If a jump pack equipped Vanguard Veteran Squad arrives from Reserve by Deep Strike, the player can elect for the squad to perform a Heroic Intervention – declaring this before the deep strike scatter dice are rolled. If he declares a Heroic Intervention, the Vanguard Veteran Squad cannot shoot (or run) that turn but can assault (provided they are close enough). This ability cannot be used if an independent character has joined the Vanguard Veteran Squad.

TERMINATOR SQUADS

Terminator armour (also known as Tactical Dreadnought Armour) is the heaviest form of battlesuit available to a Space Marine. It is the zenith of armoured protection, impenetrable to anything less than a direct hit from a lascannon. Indeed, a Terminator is so well protected that even such a dolorous strike has no certainty of causing him harm. Nor is Terminator armour simply a protective shell. Once in motion, the mass of the suit is dangerous enough by itself, for the servos and relays designed to propel the dead weight of plasteel and ceramite plates brook no interference from walls, trees or living flesh. This is not to say a Terminator must bludgeon his foe into submission. Each suit contains its own dedicated weapons systems, commonly a storm bolter and power fist or a pair of lightning claws, but such is the armour's stability and versatility that these are often exchanged for heavier weaponry. Indeed, the Terminator armour's adamantium exoskeleton is capable of supporting weapons systems considered too bulky to be wielded by power armoured troops, such as chainfists, assault cannons and the lethally effective cyclone missile launcher.

The matchless combination of protection and offensive might presented by Terminator armour is fearsome enough, yet it is the warrior inside who is by far the deadliest component. Only the most accomplished of the Blood Angels' 1st Company veterans are granted the honour of wearing a suit of Terminator armour, and nowhere is this

wealth of heroism and battle experience better put to use than when put in control of a suit of Tactical Dreadnought Armour and its death-dealing weaponry. Scant wonder is it then that Blood Angels Terminators draw the most dangerous duties and go wherever the fighting is at its thickest.

All Space Marines view suits of Terminator armour as sacred relics, and treasure them beyond any other wargear their Chapter possesses. This is in part due to the great age of the armour, but largely because of the Crux Terminatus – Ithe honour badge that sits proudly on the Terminator's left shoulder. Each Crux Terminatus, so the story goes, contains at its heart a sliver of the battle armour worn by the Emperor during his final battle with the arch-traitor Horus. Each suit of Terminator armour is therefore considered to very much be a direct extension of the Emperor's Will and honoured accordingly. Yet the suits of Terminator armour possessed by the Blood Angels are, if possible, even more revered than those in other Chapters. After all, it was Battle Brothers clad in these suits who delivered the Chapter's retribution against the Space Hulk *Sin of Damnation*, thus expunging one of the Blood Angels' most profound failures in a campaign of righteous vengeance.

	WS	BS	S	T	W	I	A	Ld	Sv
Terminator	4	4	4	4	1	4	2	9	2+
Terminator Sergeant	4	4	4	4	1	4	2	9	2+

UNIT TYPE: Infantry.

WARGEAR:
Terminator Squad only:
Terminator armour, storm bolter, power fist (the Sergeant instead has a power sword).

Terminator Assault Squad only:
Terminator armour, lightning claws.

SPECIAL RULES: And They Shall Know No Fear, Combat Squads, The Red Thirst.

"We are the Vengeance of the Blood Angels made manifest. Fear our wrath."

– Veteran Sergeant Armando, Blood Angels 1st Company

DREADNOUGHTS

A Dreadnought is death incarnate, a towering war machine whose fearsome weaponry is guided by a pilot buried deep within its shell. Whilst a Dreadnought might look like a walking tank, it is more properly described as a suit of armour, for it serves as an artificial body for its pilot, a mighty hero of the Blood Angels whose own mortal form was long ago shattered by the trials of war. Bound into the heart of the Dreadnought's sarcophagus, the pilot continues to fight against the enemies of his Chapter, his fighting spirit undimmed by the ruin of his physical body.

Each Dreadnought can be configured to carry a variety of armament, making it equally effective at anti-armour and anti-personal roles at close and distant ranges. Whilst a Dreadnought's armour-plating is not quite on par with the Chapter's main-line tanks, the instantaneous reaction time afforded by the pilot's cyborganic web is far swifter and more precise than the manual interfaces of more conventional vehicles.

Furioso Dreadnoughts

Furioso Dreadnoughts are the most venerable of all. Many bear the scars earned during the Battle for the Emperor's Palace, ten millennia ago. Some extremely rare Furioso Dreadnoughts are even guided by the crippled and ancient body of a Blood Angels Librarian. These are perhaps the most fearsome of their kind, combining as they do a Librarian's psychic might with the unyielding body of the Dreadnought.

All Furiosos are living relics, reminders of the Blood Angels' glorious past and living repositories of tradition. Even Dante, wise though he is, seeks counsel with the Chapter's Furiosos in preparation for arduous campaigns, combining their ageless insights with his own for the Chapter's greater glory.

Death Company Dreadnoughts

Even a Blood Angel wrapped in the adamantium embrace of a Dreadnought's sarcophagus is not immune to the Black Rage. It is both a blessing and a curse for an entombed brother to succumb, for whilst the Dreadnought armour greatly magnifies the lost Brother's ability to wreak havoc amongst the enemy, it also renders him near-immune to any form of restraint his Battle-Brothers might try to place upon him. So it is that a Death Company Dreadnought that survives the battle will often rampage for days afterwards until the Chapter's Techmarines can rig a device to disable it. The Sanguinary Priests can then judge whether or not the Dreadnought's occupant should be sedated until the next battle, or relieved of life's burden so that another might take his place.

WARGEAR:

Dreadnought:
Smoke launchers, multi-melta, blood fist with built-in storm bolter.

Furioso and Death Company Dreadnought:
Smoke launchers, two blood fists. One blood fist has a built-in storm bolter, the other has a built-in meltagun.

Furioso Librarian:
Smoke launchers, blood fist with built-in storm bolter, force weapon (see the Warhammer 40,000 rulebook), psychic hood (see page 46).

SPECIAL RULES:

Dreadnought and Furioso Dreadnought:
The Red Thirst.

Furioso Librarian also has:
Psyker: A Furioso Librarian is a psyker and has two psychic powers from the list given on page 63 (chosen when the army is picked). He can use one power each player turn, and counts as being Leadership 10 for all psychic purposes. If he suffers the Perils of the Warp, treat it as a glancing hit.

Death Company Dreadnought:
Fleet, Furious Charge, Rage.

None Can Stay My Wrath: A Death Company Dreadnought ignores 'crew shaken' and 'crew stunned' results.

	WS	BS	S	Armour			I	A
				F	**S**	**R**		
Dreadnought	4	4	6	12	12	10	4	2
Furioso Dreadnought	6	4	6	13	12	10	4	2(3)
Death Company Dreadnought	5	4	6	12	12	10	4	3(4)

UNIT TYPE: Vehicle, Walker.

BIKE SQUADS

The Blood Angels operate fewer Bike Squads than other Space Marine Chapters. Bikers are traditionally drafted from a Chapter's Assault Squads, and few Blood Angels are anything but reluctant to yield their jump pack for a ground-bound bike. Accordingly, the Blood Angels' bikers are often viewed by their brethren as being somewhat peculiar, for surely no true scion of Sanguinius would willingly yield the skies? In spite of this incessant stigma, or perhaps because of it, those Battle-Brothers who embrace duty in a bike squad are amongst the most accomplished practitioners of their chosen battle-craft in the Imperium, bettered in skill perhaps only by the Space Marines of the White Scars Chapter and the Dark Angels' Ravenwing.

Unable as they are to field a single unstoppable bike assault force, the Blood Angels chiefly employ their Bike Squads as fast-moving reconnaissance and ambush troops. Such units act on strategic information gathered by Thunderhawk Gunships or infiltrated Scout Squads, striking at weaknesses in the enemy lines not immediately accessible to slower-moving or more entrenched forces. Nonetheless, Blood Angels commanders are nothing if not adaptable, and have a far wider range of tactical tricks to which their Bike Squads can be set, should the theatre of war so dictate, including feint strikes, aggressive recon missions, and acting as swift-moving outrider screens for advancing Rhino and Predator armoured convoys.

As with all of the technology employed by the Blood Angels, their mechanical steeds are incredibly durable, able to perform uncomplainingly in a variety of challenging environments, from icy plains to rubble-strewn ruins, shifting desert sands to rocky moonscapes. No less important is the fact that the bikes are also simple enough in design that their riders can perform jury-rig repairs when the situation requires it. Such repairs are often needed, for the Blood Angels are infamous for pushing their bikes to the limit, forcing whatever extra speed they can out of the engines and riding at full tilt over terrain that would cripple a lesser machine in seconds. This then is the true worth of the Blood Angels' Bike Squads, for no other land unit could hope to cover so wide a variety of terrain so swiftly.

Most Bike Squads consist of ten Blood Angels bikers, eight riding conventional bikes, with the remaining two assigned to an Attack bike – a bike with a sidecar-mounted heavy weapon. Should even this formidable firepower prove insufficient to the task at hand, several Attack Bikes can be detached from their squads and forged into what is nothing less than a fast-moving Devastator Squad. Such units are feared the galaxy over as highly-effective tank-hunters. Whilst their parent squads run interference, the Attack Bikes dart forward to bring the sidecar's multi-melta into effective range, slagging enemy tanks with pinpoint volleys before spurring away from retaliative fire.

	WS	BS	S	T	W	I	A	Ld	Sv
Space Marine Biker	4	4	4	4(5)	1	4	1	8	3+
Biker Sergeant	4	4	4	4(5)	1	4	2	9	3+
Attack Bike	4	4	4	4(5)	2	4	2	8	3+

UNIT TYPE: Bikes.

WARGEAR: Power armour, bolt pistol, frag and krak grenades, Space Marine Bike. The Attack Bike also has a heavy bolter.

SPECIAL RULES: And They Shall Know No Fear, The Red Thirst.

Combat Squads: A Bike Squad chosen at full strength (for a total of eight bikes and one Attack Bike) can split into two Combat Squads as described on page 23.

Note that if this is done the Attack Bike counts as two models, giving one Combat Squad of five bikes, and one of three bikes and an Attack Bike.

"We ride upon the wings of the storm. What hope of escape can our foes possibly have?"

– Sergeant Spiccaré, Blood Angels 1st Company

SCOUT SQUADS

When new recruits are accepted into the ranks of the Blood Angels, they must first serve their time in the Chapter's Scout Company. It is the job of the Scout Company's sergeants to take these essentially untrained neophytes and transform them into full Blood Angels, ready and worthy to assume their place in the Chapter's Battle and Reserve Companies.

Over the months and years of gruelling and rigorous training, each Scout will refine his rudimentary combat skills, becoming familiar at first, and then deadly, with shotgun, bolter and combat blade. As he progresses, the Scout will master the precision of the sniper rifle, the destructive versatility of the missile launcher and the reaping roar of the heavy bolter. Only when the Scout Sergeant is convinced of the recruit's readiness will he have the chance to test his skill against the enemies of Mankind.

Unlike the more conventional Blood Angels forces, whose onslaught is deliberately bold and unconcealed, the better to intimidate and wrong-foot a foe, Scouts perform missions of a stealthier sort. They specialise in unsupported operations behind enemy lines – identifying and neutralising supply routes, ammunition dumps and command posts, ambushing reinforcement columns and sowing dismay far from the battlefront. Such missions are vital to shortening the duration of a campaign, and an excellent training ground for the Scouts.

Once a Scout has proven himself as part of a regular squad, he will be reassigned to one of the Company's Scout Bike squadrons. Service in such a unit is another vital part of a Blood Angel's training, familiarising the Scout as it does with the first of many vehicles he will be expected to master as part of his duties. Those Scouts who prove adept at controlling their mechanical steeds, and who excel at the hit and run tactics that are central to a Scout Biker's mission, will graduate straight from their Scout Biker Squad to crew assignments on a Land Speeder, or perhaps even a Baal Predator. To be accepted to such a posting so young is a great honour, and rivalry amongst Scout Bikers is therefore incredibly common. Such competitiveness can prove disastrous if left unchecked, for bravado and pride swiftly turn to recklessness, yet boldness is as much a part of a Blood Angel as is his gene-seed, and is simply one more weapon that the Scout must learn to master.

UNIT TYPE: Scouts are **Infantry.** Scout Bikers are **Bikes.**

WARGEAR:

Scouts and Scout Bikers: **Scout armour, shotgun, bolt pistol, frag and krak grenades.**

Scout Bikers only: **Space Marine Bike.**

Locator Beacon: Scouts often carry a locator beacon, a signalling package containing a teleport homer, broad-spectrum communicator and geo-positional tracking. When activated, the locator beacon uploads detailed positional information, allowing precision reinforcement.

If a unit wishes to deploy via Deep Strike and chooses to do so within 6" of a model carrying a locator beacon, then it won't scatter. Note that the locator beacon must already be on the table at the start of the turn for it to be used.

SPECIAL RULES:

Scouts and Scout Bikers: **And They Shall Know No Fear, Combat Squads, The Red Thirst, Infiltrate, Scouts.**

Scouts only: **Move Through Cover.**

	WS	BS	S	T	W	I	A	Ld	Sv
Scout	3	3	4	4	1	4	1	8	4+
Scout Sergeant	4	4	4	4	1	4	2	9	4+
Scout Biker	3	3	4	4(5)	1	4	1	8	4+
Scout Biker Sergeant	4	4	4	4(5)	1	4	2	9	4+

DROP PODS

A Drop Pod is an armoured orbital re-entry pod employed almost exclusively by the Space Marines. Each is little more than a ceramite-plated shell, bereft of all but the most rudimentary accommodations, its only purpose to swiftly deliver either a squad or a Dreadnought from an orbiting Battle Barge or Strike Cruiser into the maelstrom of battle. Drop Pods are crucial to the seek-and-destroy nature of the Space Marines' mission, allowing as they do a strike force to begin its bloody work within moments of its arrival in planetary orbit. There is little an enemy can do to prevent such an assault, or even prepare for its impact. Indeed, it is said that one could sooner stay the vengeance of an angry god than prevent an incoming Drop Pod reaching its target. All the unfortunate foe can do is marshal his warriors against the onslaught to come.

Once released, Drop Pods plummet through a planet's atmosphere at incredible velocity, speeding ever faster as the world's gravity takes hold. So fast does a Drop Pod descend that interceptor batteries and even the most agile of fighter craft have little to no chance of landing a hit, let alone of causing significant damage. Only at the very last moment does the Drop Pod's ring of retro-thrusters fire, slowing the descent and aiming the capsule onto its target. Within moments of its smouldering hull coming to rest, the Drop Pod's hatches blow open and its occupants charge into the fray, weapons blazing as they bring the vengeance of the Blood Angels upon the dazed and disoriented foe.

	Type	Armour		
		BS	F	S	R
Drop Pod	Open-topped	4	12	12	12

WARGEAR: Storm bolter.

Deathwind Launcher: Some Drop Pods are upgraded to carry a deathwind launcher in place of a storm bolter:

Range	Strength	AP	Type
12"	5	-	Heavy 1, Large Blast

TRANSPORT:

The Drop Pod has a transport capacity of 10 models. It can instead transport a single Dreadnought.

Once the Drop Pod has landed, the hatches are blown and all passengers must immediately disembark as normal. Once passengers have disembarked, no models can embark on the Drop Pod for the remainder of the game.

Fire Points and Access Points: Once deployed, the Drop Pod is no longer a sealed environment and is therefore counted as being open-topped.

SPECIAL RULES:

Drop Pod Assault: Drop Pods always enter play using the Deep Strike rules from the Mission Special Rules section of the Warhammer 40,000 rulebook. At the beginning of your first turn, you must choose half of your Drop Pods (rounding up) to make a 'Drop Pod Assault'. Units making a Drop Pod Assault arrive on the player's first turn. The arrival of the remaining Drop Pods is rolled for as normal. A unit that Deep Strikes via Drop Pod cannot assault in the turn it arrives.

Inertial Guidance System: Should a Drop Pod scatter on top of impassable terrain or another model (friend or foe!) then reduce the scatter distance by the minimum required in order to avoid the obstacle.

Immobile: A Drop Pod cannot move once it has entered the battle, and counts in all respects as a vehicle that has suffered an immobilised damage result (which cannot be repaired in any way).

"No angel ever descended from the heavens with as much sound and fury as do we. Let the Drop Pods' roar herald our coming – the brief warning our foe hears shall avail them naught."

– Sergeant Drusani, Blood Angels 1st Company

LAND SPEEDERS

The Land Speeder is a light combat skimmer, commonly deployed as a support craft for the main strike force. Whilst not capable of flight in the truest sense, the Land Speeder is able to generate an anti-gravitational field, allowing it to perform low-altitude manoeuvres or even a controlled descent from the upper atmosphere. Whilst not as swift as a conventional atmosphere-capable fighter-craft, the Land Speeder is far more nimble. By altering the shape and vector of their Land Speeder's anti-grav field, the crew can throw their vehicle into a variety of death-defying manoeuvres, performing vertical dives or threading high-speed courses beneath a jungle canopy. Such feats require not only a robust and responsive vehicle – which the Land Speeder undoubtedly is – but also inhuman nerves and reactions on the part of the pilot, explaining perhaps why Land Speeders have for so long remained scarce outside of Space Marine Chapters, and are chiefly absent in other wings of the Imperium's military.

As with most vehicles employed by the Blood Angels, the Land Speeder can be outfitted with a variety of weaponry, determined by the needs of the mission. A reconnaissance craft will normally only be equipped with a heavy bolter for self defence – although its real defence is a lightning-fast withdrawal. Heavier loadouts abound, turning the Land Speeder into an infantry-reaping attack craft, dedicated tank-hunter or a balance of both.

The Land Speeder's only real weakness is its lack of armour plating. Nonetheless, Land Speeders have a knack for surviving battles in which more formidable vehicles perish. Their manoeuvrability can be considered the chief reason for this. It is no easy thing to hit a swiftly moving Land Speeder at the best of times, and almost impossible if the crew is aware of their danger. That said, it is not uncommon for enemies to be deceived by a Land Speeder's lack of armour and comparatively small size, assuming it to be less of a threat than the other forces arrayed against him. So it is that volleys capable of reducing a Land Speeder to so much scrap metal are often wasted against heavily armoured Predators or Vindicators, allowing the Land Speeder to continue its mission unhindered.

The Blood Angels consider Land Speeders to be vital support craft, capable as they are of swiftly redeploying whilst providing formidable supporting fire. As it is not unheard of for a Blood Angels assault element to outstrip the strike force's more static fire support, such as Devastator Squads and Predator tanks, having a handful of what are essentially fast-reaction weapons platforms can mean the difference between victory and defeat. This being the case, Land Speeders – and their pilots – are in almost constant demand, with the various strike force commanders keeping a keen eye on Chapter deployments in order to snap up any Land Speeders whose assignments have come to an end.

This constant warfooting inevitably takes a heavy toll on even the Land Speeder's robust mechanisms and machinery. Thusly, battlefield repairs are common – wherever a Blood Angels Land Speeder goes, a Techmarine can inevitably be found close by.

			Armour		
	Type	BS	F	S	R
Land Speeder	Skimmer, Fast	4	10	10	10

WARGEAR: Heavy bolter.

Typhoon Missile Launcher: The typhoon is a multiple missile launcher that uses an array of highly-sophisticated targeters to ensure its payload strikes where it can do the most damage.

The typhoon missile launcher is equipped with both frag and krak missiles. Declare which type of missile you wish to use each time the typhoon missile launcher fires.

Frag Missiles

Range	Strength	AP	Type
48"	4	6	Heavy 2, Blast

Krak Missiles

Range	Strength	AP	Type
48"	8	3	Heavy 2

SPECIAL RULES: Deep Strike.

RHINOS

The Blood Angels consider the Rhino armoured transport to be amongst the most crucial of all their tools of war. With its durable chassis, armoured hull and almost endlessly reliable power system, the Rhino is ideally suited for the fast-moving combat stance employed by the Blood Angels. Indeed, the Rhino's balance of armour, speed and transport capacity render it equally invaluable during swift redeployments, strategic strikes and armoured advances.

The Rhino's ruggedness is chief amongst the traits that make it so valued, a throwback to the vehicle's origins as a colonial exploration vehicle. Every Rhino contains various fail-safe and backup systems in case of damage, as well as automatic self-repair technology. Even unsupervised, these repair systems can, given time, bypass all but the heaviest damage to the Rhino's motive units. When overseen by a skilled crew, a seemingly crippled Rhino can regain mobility in mere minutes – a most useful trait for a battlefield transport.

Proof positive of the Rhino's durability can be taken from the age of the vehicles serving in the Blood Angels armoury. Fully half the Rhinos therein are more than five thousand years old, with two yet surviving that served in the campaigns of Sanguinius himself, ten millennia ago. It need not be said that the Blood Angels are incredibly protective of these honoured veterans and fight all the harder in their august presence.

Naturally, the Rhino is not used exclusively by the Blood Angels, or even by the Space Marines as a whole. At one time it was the principle transport vehicle of the Imperium's armed forces, and though not as widespread as once it was, the Rhino still sees a great deal of use across the galaxy. However, it can be truly said that the specific design of Rhino used by the Blood Angels – known as the Lucifer pattern, for the Techmarine who pioneered its creation – is unique to the Chapter.

The Blood Angels Rhino incorporates many of the design upgrades present in the Baal Predator in order to greatly increase the Rhino's speed and mobility. Although these alterations are relatively recent, the Chapter's Techmarines had long experimented with different methods of overcharging their Rhino's engines, but all such trials proved to be unreliable at best, and disastrous at worst. It wasn't until the unique challenges of the Second War for Armageddon forced a new approach that the attempt was made to merge the traditional design with that of the Baal Predator. So successful was the altered configuration that it was swiftly rolled out to the Chapter's entire complement of Rhinos, as well as other tanks founded on the same design, such as the Vindicator and Razorback.

	Type	Armour		
		BS	F	S	R
Rhino	Tank, Fast	4	11	11	10

Note that all Blood Angels Rhinos (and Rhino variants shown opposite) have specially modified 'Lucifer' engines unique to the Blood Angels Chapter.

Lucifer engines grant the vehicle the 'fast' vehicle type as included in each of the characteristic profiles.

WARGEAR: Storm bolter, smoke launchers.

TRANSPORT:
The Rhino has a transport capacity of ten models. It cannot carry models in Terminator armour.

Fire Points: Two models can fire from the Rhino's top hatch.

Access Points: A Rhino has one access point on each side of the hull and one at the rear.

SPECIAL RULES:
Repair: Rhinos are exceptionally resilient and easy to maintain. As a result they can often be repaired by their crew in the heat of battle.

If a Rhino is immobilised for any reason, then in subsequent turns the crew can attempt a temporary repair instead of the vehicle shooting. Roll a D6 in the Shooting phase – on a roll of a 6, the Rhino is no longer immobilised.

RAZORBACKS

The Razorback is a heavily-armed variant of the Rhino that sacrifices a portion of its transport capacity for a twin-linked turret weapon.

The Razorback is commonly deployed as a support vehicle for Rhino-transported squads, where its superior firepower greatly increases the strike force's effectiveness without overly compromising mobility. Another common strategy is to deploy Razorback-mounted squads as mobile outriders for the Chapter's armoured assaults.

WARGEAR: Twin-linked heavy bolter, smoke launchers.

TRANSPORT:

Six models. The Razorback cannot carry models in Terminator armour.

Fire Points: None

Access Points: One access point on each side of the hull and one at the rear.

	Type	BS	Armour F	S	R
Razorback	Tank, Fast	4	11	11	10

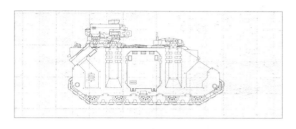

"Let the night sky shine with our vengeance."

– Brother Sorin, Armourer

PREDATORS

The Predator is the Blood Angels' main battle tank. It completely surrenders transport capacity for much improved frontal armour, a heavy turret-mounted armament and, commonly, sponson-mounted support weaponry.

The Predator, in particular, benefits greatly from the Lucifer pattern modifications, with the reverse-engineered heat sinks and recoil suppressors from the Baal design drastically increasing the Predator's rate of fire whilst on the move.

WARGEAR
Autocannon, smoke launchers.

	Type	BS	Armour F	S	R
Predator	Tank, Fast	4	13	11	10

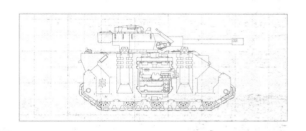

WHIRLWINDS

The Whirlwind is a tracked suppression battery, a lightly armoured tank capable of raining precision missile fire down upon enemy positions. So sophisticated are the Whirlwind's targeting systems that they allow the tank to maintain a deadly accurate barrage even when the enemy are not in plain sight. Though the Blood Angels prefer to fight their battles at extreme close quarters, few Captains deem their strike forces to be properly equipped unless at least a single Whirlwind is present.

WARGEAR
Whirlwind multiple missile launcher, smoke launchers.

	Type	BS	Armour F	S	R
Whirlwind	Tank, Fast	4	11	11	10

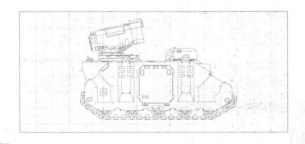

VINDICATORS

Since its inception, the Vindicator has been host to innumerable alterations but has always retained its fearsome short-range weaponry. Whether fighting in the vanguard of a spearhead or pounding an enemy fortress into dust, the Vindicator is a terrifying foe. Never is this truer than when a Vindicator is in the hands of a Blood Angels crew, who take delight in spurring their tanks forwards at high speed in order to unleash the fury of the demolisher cannon at lethal point-blank range.

WARGEAR
Demolisher cannon, storm bolter, smoke launchers.

	Type	BS	Armour F	S	R
Vindicator	Tank, Fast	4	13	11	10

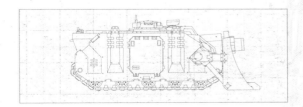

BAAL PREDATORS

The Baal Predator is a specialised variant of the Predator design, used only by the Blood Angels and their Successor Chapters. It has been in service with the Chapter since the earliest days of the Great Crusade, when the Blood Angels seized its Standard Template Construct from a ruined archeotech vault. In a move that was riven with controversy even then, the victorious Blood Angels did not hand the template over to the Adeptus Mechanicus, despite the dark threats directed at them, but brought it back to Baal to take its place amongst the Chapter's other relics.

The discovery of the Baal Predator design proved incredibly fortuitous for the Blood Angels. An example of a later generation of Predator design, with an armament of a twin-linked, turret-mounted assault cannon, backed up by heavy flamer or heavy bolter sponsons, the Baal's weapon load-out was far more closely suited to the close range fire fights of the Blood Angels than the more traditional configurations ever were. Furthermore, the Baal Predator was also capable of much greater speed and manoeuvrability than previous iterations – a trait whole-heartedly embraced by the Blood Angels and ultimately reverse-engineered and applied to many of the Chapter's other tanks by its Techmarines.

Due to its unique configuration, a Baal Predator is far more heavily armed and armoured than other vehicles of a similar size and speed. Accordingly, Baal Predators are commonly used as vanguard units, operating far ahead of the main

Blood Angels army, shredding the enemy's forward patrols, or looping around the front line to strike at ammo dumps, fuel stores or other vital targets. In smaller engagements, a Baal might well be deployed in support of one or two Tactical or Assault Squads. Here, its armament will often be further augmented to the task at hand. A Baal Predator equipped with a turret-mounted flamestorm cannon is a tried and tested method of clearing bunkers and barricades, whilst the addition of sponsons to the basic chassis can massively reinforce the basic firepower.

Given the Baal Predator's success and versatility within the Chapter's strike forces, it is little wonder, perhaps, that the Blood Angels are even more protective of these vehicles than others in their armoury. This sense of watchful custodianship is only heightened by the presence of Adeptus Mechanicus emissaries lurking like vultures on the periphery of any campaign where a Baal Predator is deployed. The Tech-Priests have never forgiven what they view as the Blood Angels' theft of the design, and would dearly love to lay their hands on even a wrecked Baal Predator and so reclaim its technological secrets for the brotherhood of the Machine God.

Thus far, relations between the Blood Angels and the Adeptus Mechanicus have remained peaceful, if perhaps somewhat less than that of steadfast allies, but who can tell what the future will bring?

			Armour		
	Type	BS	F	S	R
Baal Predator	Tank, Fast	4	13	11	10

WARGEAR: Twin-linked assault cannon, smoke launchers.

Flamestorm Cannon: A flamestorm cannon is a colossal flame projector that sends a billowing tide of burning promethium into the thick of the foe. Cover is no defence against its wrath, and only the thickest armour can hope to offer any protection.

Range	Strength	AP	Type
Template	6	3	Heavy 1

SPECIAL RULES: Scouts.

LAND RAIDERS

Though its ancient origins lie shrouded by the mists of time, the Land Raider remains the single most destructive and versatile tank at the Blood Angels' command. Inside its bonded ceramite and adamantium hull, the Land Raider has a sealed-environment transport capacity sufficient for a full ten-man squad of Space Marines, their field supplies, communications gear, munitions and medical facilities.

Over the centuries, differing Land Raider configurations have been accepted into the Blood Angels armoury. Most of these variations on the basic Land Raider design have fallen out of favour with the Blood Angels, having proved too temperamental or unsuitable for the Blood Angels' way of war, but two: the Land Raider Crusader and Land Raider Redeemer, have been embraced with all the enthusiasm of the original design. The Land Raider Crusader's murderous hurricane bolters and the fury of the Redeemer's flamestorm cannons are well-loved by the Blood Angels – few Space Marines appreciate the finer tactical uses of short range firepower more than the Scions of Sanguinius.

There is only one shortcoming that the Blood Angels have been able to identify with the Land Raider design – try as they might, the Chapter's Techmarines cannot find a way to boost, overcharge or otherwise improve its engines. Unable to customise the Land Raider so it can keep pace with the Chapter's Lucifer-powered Rhinos, the Blood Angels use Thunderhawk Transporters to drop them directly into the heart of the battle, trusting to the tank's sturdy nature to allow a safe landing for it and its crew. This a risky ploy, to be sure, but one that swiftly proves its worth when the Land Raider's formidable armament opens up against an ill-defended enemy position.

	Type	Armour BS	Armour F	Armour S	Armour R
Land Raider	Tank	4	14	14	14

WARGEAR:
Land Raider:
Two twin-linked lascannons, one twin-linked heavy bolter, smoke launchers.

Land Raider Crusader:
Two hurricane bolters, one twin-linked assault cannon, smoke launchers, frag assault launchers.

Land Raider Redeemer:
Two flamestorm cannons, one twin-linked assault cannon, smoke launchers, frag assault launchers.

TRANSPORT: Land Raiders have a transport capacity of **ten models. Land Raider Crusaders** have a transport capacity of **sixteen models. Land Raider Redeemers** have a transport capacity of **twelve models.**

Fire Points: None.

Access Points: A Land Raider has one access point on each side of the hull and one at its front.

SPECIAL RULES:
Deep Strike. A unit that Deep Strikes via a Land Raider cannot assault in the turn it arrives.

Power of the Machine Spirit: The vehicle can fire one more weapon than would normally be permitted. In addition, this weapon can be fired at a different target unit to any other weapons, subject to the normal rules for shooting. Therefore, a vehicle that has moved at combat speed can fire two weapons, and a vehicle that has either moved at cruising speed, or has suffered a 'Crew Stunned' or 'Crew Shaken' result can fire a single weapon.

Assault Vehicle: Models disembarking from any access point on a Land Raider can launch an assault on the turn they do so. Note that a unit that Deep Strikes within a Land Raider cannot assault in the turn it arrives.

STORMRAVEN GUNSHIPS

The Stormraven Gunship is a relatively new addition to the Blood Angels armoury. Like its larger and more established brother, the Thunderhawk, the Stormraven is an extremely versatile craft that combines the role of dropship, armoured transport and strike aircraft.

The introduction of the Stormraven lies shrouded in secrecy. It has been reported that its Standard Template Construct file was discovered at the start of the 41st Millennium in a forgotten Martian archive, and that the Adeptus Mechanicus refused to begin mass-production until they assured themselves that the schematics were hale, untainted and utterly in keeping with the strictures and covenants of the Machine God. Nonetheless, some records suggest that the Stormraven was in existence even before then, most notably active in the service of the Grey Knights, the secretive Daemon-hunters of Titan. Who can say where the truth of the Stormraven's provenance lies, for the Imperium's bureaucracy is as labyrinthine as it is petty. It is just as believable that shadow-politics and administrative inertia are behind the Stormraven's belated introduction into the armies of Mankind as it is that the delay was caused only by diligence on the part of the Adeptus Mechanicus.

The Stormraven is not only smaller than a Thunderhawk but, thanks to its array of vectored thrusters, is also considerably more agile. This, combined with the precise skill and incredible reaction time of its Space Marine crew, allows it to jink effortlessly through the interceptor fire and manoeuvre at full speed through the cluttered spires of a hive city. As a result, the Blood Angels employ Stormravens as air support craft in environs where it would be foolish or impractical for a Thunderhawk to attempt the same role. Other Chapters might take a different tack altogether, using Drop Pods or Land Raiders to achieve the same strategic goals, but the Blood Angels refuse to cede their mastery of the heavens to any foe, even for a moment.

The mission role of a strike force's Stormraven Gunships varies greatly from battlezone to battlezone and, to an extent, the personality of the strike force commander. Most prefer to employ their Stormravens in place of other transports, combining as they do the swift orbital descent of the Drop Pod with the battlefield versatility of a Rhino or Razorback. Fully twelve power-armoured Space Marines can be accommodated in the Stormraven's adamantium belly, ready to charge out of the gunship once the assault ramp clangs down, or make an aerial descent via grav chutes should a landing not be possible. Furthermore, the Stormraven can also carry a mighty Dreadnought in its rear cargo grapples – the smallest craft able to do so. Yet to use the Stormraven as a transport alone is to overlook its formidable weapons array which, whilst varying greatly from gunship to gunship, is easily the equal of the Chapter's most potent land-based fighting vehicles, and more than capable of wreaking untold destruction.

	Type	BS	Armour F	S	R
Stormraven	Skimmer, Fast	4	12	12	12

WARGEAR: Twin-linked heavy bolter, twin-linked assault cannon, and four bloodstrike missiles.

Bloodstrike Missiles: Bloodstrike missiles have a two-stage solid fuel booster, designed to deliver a punishing blow to an enemy tank. Each missile can only be fired once per game.

Range	Strength	AP	Type
72"	8	1	Heavy 1, One shot

Ceramite Plating: The Stormraven's hull plates are designed to protect it from the extreme conditions of orbital re-entry, but they also serve to thwart the fury of certain weapons. Melta weapons do not gain the extra D6 armour penetration when shooting at a Stormraven Gunship.

TRANSPORT:
The Stormraven can carry two separate squads: one unit of up to 12 models in its cabin, plus a single Dreadnought in its rear grapples (if the Stormraven explodes, the Dreadnought will suffer a Strength 4 hit on its rear armour). Unlike other transports, the Stormraven can carry jump infantry (each takes up two points of transport capacity). For the purposes of claiming/contesting objectives and embarking/disembarking from a Stormraven, measure to and from its base. For example, a unit wishing to embark a Stormraven can do so if, at the end of their Movement, all models in the unit are within 2" of the Stormraven's base.

Fire Points: None.

Access Points: A Stormraven has one access point at the front of its hull, one on either side and another at the rear.

SPECIAL RULES: Deep Strike.

Assault Vehicle: Models disembarking from a Stormraven can launch an assault on the turn they do so (providing the Stormraven did not deep strike).

Power of the Machine Spirit (see page 37).

Skies of Blood: If the Stormraven has moved flat out, passengers can still disembark, but they must do so as follows. Nominate any point over which the Stormraven moved over and deploy the squad as if it were deep striking onto that point. If the unit scatters, every model must immediately take a Dangerous Terrain test. Models with jump packs can make a more controlled descent – not only do they not take Dangerous Terrain tests (unless they do land in Dangerous Terrain), they can use the Descent of Angels special rule to make a more accurate landing. If any of the models cannot be deployed, the unit is destroyed as described in the 1-2 result on the Deep Strike Mishap table. Note that models that disembark in this manner cannot assault on the turn they do so.

TECHMARINES

Techmarines are the Blood Angels' war-smiths. They are responsible for the creation and maintenance of all the Chapter's weapons, from bolter shells to towering defence lasers. Without the knowledge of the Techmarines, the Blood Angels would swiftly fade into history, for what good is a Space Marine's strong right arm and implacable will if he does not have a starship to bear him forth to worlds where his might is needed?

Every twenty years the Chapter's Techmarines walk amongst their Battle-Brothers, gauging which amongst the assembled ranks have the talent and skill to join their enigmatic brotherhood. There is a never a shortage of suitable candidates, for the manipulation of technology is merely another form of artistry, and the Blood Angels have ever shown aptitude and enthusiasm for all manner of arts. It is for this reason perhaps that the Blood Angels are said to have some of the most skilled Techmarines and artificers of any Chapter, their love of elegance and sophistication given over to new fields of endeavour. This innate craftsmanship serves the novitiate Techmarines well during their initiation to the arcana of technology.

It is not on Baal, but on the red planet of Mars that the Techmarines learn their trade, brought into the mysteries of the Machine God by his foremost adherents, the Adeptus Mechanicus. Whatever the resentment the Adeptus of Mars might feel towards the Blood Angels regarding the 'theft' of the Baal Predator template, the ancient pacts between Chapter and Machine Cult endure – unsurprising perhaps as it was at the Emperor's command that the accords were first forged, and neither party would think to question his will. Under the tuition of the Adeptus Mechanicus, the novitiate Techmarines are immersed in the preciously guarded lore of technology – the rites of maintenance and battlefield repair; rituals of forging and creation; hymnals of awakening and invigoration. When his training is complete, a Techmarine can visit miracles upon ailing technology, bringing new life to crippled vehicles and weaponry with but a touch and, if given time or accompanied by enough suitably equipped Servitors, repairing the seemingly irreparable. Such skill makes a Techmarine a valued comrade upon the battlefield, and is more than sufficient cause for his uninitiated Battle-Brothers to overlook his dual loyalties to the Chapter and the Machine God.

	WS	BS	S	T	W	I	A	Ld	Sv
Techmarine	4	4	4	4	1	4	1	8	2+
Servitor	3	3	3	3	1	3	1	8	4+

UNIT TYPE: Infantry.

WARGEAR:
Techmarine only:
Artificer armour, boltgun or bolt pistol, servo-arm (see page 58), frag and krak grenades.

Servitor only:
Servo-arm, close combat weapon.

SPECIAL RULES:
Techmarine only:
And They Shall Know No Fear.

Blessing of the Omnissiah: If a Techmarine is in base contact with a damaged vehicle during the Shooting phase, he can attempt to repair it instead of firing. Roll a D6 and add the following modifiers:

Each Servitor with a servo-arm in the unit	+1
The Techmarine has a servo-harness	+1

If the result is 5 or more, then either a Weapon Destroyed result or Immobilised result (owning player's choice) will be repaired. If a Weapon Destroyed result is repaired, that weapon can be fired in the following friendly Shooting phase. The Techmarine cannot repair if gone to ground or falling back.

Bolster Defences: Techmarines can increase the effectiveness of cover, reinforcing crumbling walls and re-welding badly-damaged spars. Each Techmarine can bolster a single ruin before the game begins. When you deploy, nominate one ruin in your deployment area for your Techmarine to bolster. The ruin's cover save is increased by one for the duration of the game. For example, a normal ruin (4+ save) so reinforced would offer a 3+ cover save. A ruin can only be bolstered once.

CAPTAINS

In keeping with the dictates of the Codex Astartes, the Blood Angels traditionally maintain ten Captains – one to command each of the Chapter's ten companies. That said, the actual number of Captains can briefly fall as vacancies are caused by death, or even rise as brevet captaincies are temporarily instated to grant a senior sergeant authority over a strike force. Once elevated, it is unthinkable that a Captain should be demoted for matters of incompetence – after all a Captain is no mere commander or tactician, but a paragon of duty and courage whose example serves to guide his Battle-Brothers. Accordingly, it is not unknown for Dante and the Chapter Council to occasionally delay the replacement of a fallen Brother-Captain in order to ensure that the proper promotion is made.

It is rare for the entire Chapter to fight as one, and its companies often strive in separate, far-flung wars. So then are the Blood Angels' Captains entrusted with a level of autonomy for which many other Imperial Commanders would give their eye-teeth. Yet this freedom brings weighty burdens of its own.

Each battle the Blood Angels conduct is no mere skirmish, but a crucial fight in the larger struggle for Mankind's survival. In such conflicts there can be no such thing as a minor defeat – each world lost and every scrap of territory abandoned brings the Imperium one step closer to annihilation. So too, the Captain is responsible for the lives of the Battle-Brothers under his command. Each Blood Angel lost to the tide of war is a terrible wound from which the Chapter must recover – if their lives are to be sacrificed on the altar of war, it cannot be for anything less than the most noble and deserving of causes.

Captains are the Blood Angels' foremost warriors and commanders. Indeed, it is no exaggeration to suggest that they are amongst the most dangerous and capable warriors ever to stand in defence of Mankind. Each has the combat skills and reflexes to which only a Space Marine can aspire, tempered by service amid gruelling wars and star-spanning campaigns. Yet a Captain is no mere brawler. Each can draw upon decades, even centuries, of personal combat experience to guide his actions and strategies, taking in the needs and challenges of even the most challenging of battlefield with what must appear to lesser beings as the most superficial appraisal.

A Captain is thus a truly mighty warrior who aspires to the most incredible of deeds, whether personally striving in the thick of the fray, or serving as the supreme architect of some grand military strategy. He is defeated only in death and, even then, another of his Battle-Brothers will step forward to claim the fallen mantle and thus continue the battle in the Emperor's name.

	WS	BS	S	T	W	I	A	Ld	Sv
Captain	6	5	4	4	3	5	3	10	3+

UNIT TYPE: Infantry.

WARGEAR: Power armour, boltgun or bolt pistol, chainsword, frag and krak grenades, Iron Halo.

Iron Halo: An Iron Halo incorporates a powerful energy field that can turn aside even the most deadly attacks. It confers a 4+ invulnerable save upon the bearer.

SPECIAL RULES: And They Shall Know No Fear, Independent Character.

"How do I prove my allegiance? I have trodden the blood-choked dust of ten thousand worlds, and there delivered the souls of countless millions into oblivion's embrace. What other devotion could I possibly make to prove my dedication?"

– Captain Phaeton, Blood Angels 7th Company

CAPTAIN TYCHO

Brother-Captain Erasmus Tycho was once the greatest strike leader the Blood Angels have ever known, rumoured to be Dante's protégé and chosen successor. Now he stands as a grim reminder that even the Chapter's brightest and best are not safe from the clutches of the Black Rage.

Tycho took command of the Blood Angels 3rd Company when his predecessor was slain during the Second War for Armageddon. The former sergeant swiftly proved his mettle, orchestrating the rout of Boss Grakka's Speed Freeks, and recapturing key defensive positions along the River Chaeron. Enheartened by their successes, the 3rd Company pushed on, striking at the Ork supply lines from Armageddon Prime.

It was on such a mission that Tycho and his company were ambushed. Though the Blood Angels triumphed, their Captain fell victim to an Ork Weirdboy's psychic assault early in the battle and was left for dead. Somehow, no one quite knows how, Tycho survived, but the after-effects of the terrible psychic onslaught had paralysed half of his face, freezing it forever in a terrible rictus grin. Tycho's obsession with fine aesthetic taste and beauty was as great as that of any other Blood Angel, and to him such a fate was worse than death itself. So it was that bitterness and rage began to creep into Tycho's once-pure heart, opening the door to the pent-up anger that lay at the core of Tycho's very being.

Unable to bear the pitiful looks of his Battle-Brothers, Tycho ordered the Chapter's most revered artificer to forge a mask to cover his disfigurement. This simple act seemed to grant Tycho a measure of peace and, for a time, he regained his old composure. For the remainder of the Armageddon campaign, the Blood Angels' 3rd Company stood in the thick of the fighting, Tycho directing their efforts as he had in the early stages, though none could deny that an increased fervour stole over the Captain whenever he tasted the tang of Ork blood upon the air.

In the wake of that great campaign, it swiftly became apparent that all was not right with Tycho. No longer could he relax in the hallowed halls of the Chapter Fortress, for its beauty served only to remind him of his own mutilation. Dante reluctantly assigned Tycho to permanent battle duty, yet even there he was ever more violent of temperament and attitude, and his tactics became audacious to the point of foolhardiness. Finally, as another great war began to brew on Armageddon, Tycho at last succumbed to the Black Rage and took his place in the Death Company. And it was on Armageddon, where perhaps he should have perished long before, that he finally fell, tearing at the Ork defenders of Hive Tempestora with the fury of a man possessed.

	WS	BS	S	T	W	I	A	Ld	Sv
Captain Tycho	6	5	4	4	3	5	3	10	2+
Death Company Tycho	7	4	4	4	3	5	4	8	2+

Note that there are two different profiles for Captain Tycho, one for the relatively sane Captain, and one to represent Tycho following his induction into the Death Company (and of course you may only field one of them in your force).

UNIT TYPE: Infantry.

WARGEAR: Artificer armour, bolt pistol, frag and krak grenades, Iron Halo.

Blood Song: Blood Song is a combi-melta that can use the special issue ammunition described on page 27.

The Dead Man's Hand: Tycho's close combat attacks ignore armour saves and roll an additional D6 for armour penetration. The Dead Man's Hand also includes a set of digital weapons, allowing Tycho to re-roll a single failed roll to wound in each Assault phase.

SPECIAL RULES:
Captain Tycho:
And They Shall Know No Fear, Independent Character, Preferred Enemy: Orks.

Rites of Battle: If Captain Tycho is on the battlefield, all other friendly Blood Angels units use his Leadership for Morale and Pinning tests.

SPECIAL RULES:
Death Company Tycho:
Black Rage (see page 44), Fearless, Feel No Pain, Fleet, Furious Charge, Preferred Enemy: Orks, Relentless.

CHAPLAINS

Chaplains are the foremost spiritual guardians of the Blood Angels. They preserve the Chapter's innermost secrets, vouchsafe its creed and maintain an eternal vigil for the onset of the Black Rage amongst their Battle-Brothers. In war, the Chaplains are fearsome battle-priests clad in forbidding jet-black armour crowned with skull-helms and death masks. Everything about a Chaplain's appearance and demeanour is crafted to evoke a grim reminder of mortality, to better instil dread in the foe and spur his Battle-Brothers to ever greater deeds before death takes them.

When on the battlefield, a Chaplain's place is ever at the heart of the fighting, taking joy in the carnage as only a warrior doing the most righteous of works can. Every strike of the Chaplain's skull-headed Crozius is accompanied by a line from a war-hymn or battle-prayer, rendering each blow a heartfelt offering to Primarch and Emperor. Such strident and destructive piety serves to embolden nearby Battle-Brothers, exhorting them to forget their fears and win the day for the glory of the Chapter.

The Reclusiarchs – the highest ranking Chaplains – are the keepers of the Chapter's Reclusiam, the Blood Angels' most sacred shrine. The Reclusiam nestles in the heart of a great spire that stands tall over the rest of the fortress monastery and only the tower of the Sanguinary Priesthood stands as high. No part of the fortress monastery is as revered as the Reclusiam, adorned as it is with banners and relics of ages past, its sable stones steeped in history and grandeur. Here do the Chaplains conduct their ceremonies, the rites of Initiation, Vindication and Redemption, the Blood Pact and the Host-throng. In earlier days, the Reclusiam tower was once given over to Sanguinius' quarters and the Blood Angels believe that their beloved Primarch can hear any prayer given voice within.

A small antechamber lies to the north of the Reclusiam, a sealed vault to which only the members of the Chapter Council have access. Herein are kept the Scrolls of Sanguinius, the sacred texts recorded by the Primarch during his long life, and whose secrets are said to contain vital information regarding all the terrible times to come. Here also are kept the rosters of the Chapter's deeds, records of its great victories and the legends of its mighty heroes. They are partially maintained out of pride and tradition, these weighty tomes of blood-inked parchment, but also for a more practical reason – if a Battle-Brother knows not the deeds of his Chapter's past, how can he hope to make accurate measure of his own achievements? For a Blood Angel, parity of honour with his forebears is as important as that of his peers. Thus does each Battle Brother strive to prove himself beneath the gaze of the Chapter's Chaplains, that he might one day be held as an example to the generations of Blood Angels yet to come.

	WS	BS	S	T	W	I	A	Ld	Sv
Reclusiarch	5	5	4	4	3	5	3	10	3+
Chaplain	5	4	4	4	2	4	2	10	3+

UNIT TYPE: Infantry.

WARGEAR: Power armour, boltgun or bolt pistol, frag and krak grenades.

Rosarius: A Rosarius is a gorget or amulet worn by a Chaplain. Though primarily a spiritual relic, the rosarius contains a small but powerful conversion field that protects the Chaplain from physical and spiritual harm.

A Rosarius confers a 4+ invulnerable save.

Crozius Arcanum: The Crozius Arcanum is a Space Marine Chaplain's rod of office. It is a power weapon.

SPECIAL RULES: Independent Character.

Honour of the Chapter: A Chaplain utterly embodies the honour of the Chapter. He, and all members of a squad he has joined, are fearless, as described in the Warhammer 40,000 rulebook.

Liturgies of Blood: On a player turn in which he assaults, a Chaplain and all members of any squad he has joined can re-roll failed rolls To Hit. Models in a Death Company can also re-roll failed rolls To Wound (their rage makes them particularly susceptible to the Chaplain's fiery oratory).

LEMARTES, GUARDIAN OF THE LOST

Chaplain Lemartes fell to the Black Rage amidst the preparations to liberate Hadriath XI. Unlike the other warriors of the Death Company who spearheaded the planetstrike, Lemartes survived the initial landings and, seemingly unstoppable, carved a bloody path through the Ork defenders. Only when the battle was won did the Chaplain finally collapse from his wounds. He was brought to the field Apothecarium inside the now-captured fortress, there to await the arrival of the Astorath, Redeemer of the Lost, and receive the gift of final redemption.

Yet when Astorath arrived to deliver the Chaplain into death's embrace, Lemartes demanded to live, to smite the Emperor's enemies as long as he were able. Such a thing was unheard of. Though Lemartes' eyes were bloodshot and his muscles taught with fury, his words were clear and cogent. Whilst members of the Death Company were often so deranged that Astorath had to best them in combat before he could take their lives, never before had one challenged him in so lucid a fashion. Quashing all dissent, Astorath ordered the Chaplain placed in stasis and returned to Baal until the Chapter's Librarians and Sanguinary Priests could make full examination of him.

This investigation took several months, time in which Lemartes was largely kept in the chill embrace of stasis to ensure the safety of those around him, but the results seemed to reinforce Astorath's hopes. Lemartes was unquestionably in the grip of the Black Rage, for all the physical signs were there. Yet his mind was not riven with insanity – through an act of incredible willpower, the Chaplain appeared able to hold his madness in check. Several Sanguinary Priests argued that this was but a temporary respite, and that Lemartes would succumb to the uttermost depths of madness once removed from stasis, but Astorath was not so sure. Refusing to slay Lemartes, as some of the Sanguinary Priests wished, he awoke the Chaplain from his enforced slumber and offered him a way in which he could continue to serve.

So did Lemartes become the Guardian of the Lost, the warden of the Death Company. He has repaid Astorath's faith a thousand times over, for the Death Company have never been so potent a force as they have under his guidance, their modern glories eclipsing deeds of legend. He leads his charges to ever greater renown, ensuring that the dread sacrifice of the Blood Angels' Death Company is never in vain. At battle's end, Lemartes is placed in stasis once more, to slumber through the weeks and months until his bloody talents are required again. For Lemartes, there is no longer any calm before the storm. His life is one of constant battle, for he is awoken when needed and preserved when he is not.

Lemartes is surely living on borrowed time, for even his formidable willpower cannot keep the Black Rage at bay indefinitely. Yet for the moment at least, the Chaplain's iron will holds firm. He is a symbol of hope to a Chapter slipping into the darkness, for if Lemartes can continue to reason and serve his Chapter within the dark insanity of the Black Rage, perhaps others can do so too...

	WS	BS	S	T	W	I	A	Ld	Sv
Lemartes	5	4	4	4	2	6	2	10	3+

UNIT TYPE: Jump Infantry.

WARGEAR: Power armour, bolt pistol, frag and krak grenades, jump pack, Rosarius (see page 42).

The Blood Crozius: Said to be the weapon of the very first Blood Angel High Chaplain, the Blood Crozius was given into Lemartes' keeping by Astorath the Grim.

The Blood Crozius is a master-crafted power weapon.

SPECIAL RULES: Black Rage (see page 44), Fearless, Descent of Angels, Feel No Pain, Furious Charge, Relentless.

Liturgies of Blood: On a player turn in which they assault, Lemartes and his Death Company can re-roll failed rolls to hit and to wound.

Fury Unbound: if a foe harms Lemartes, the Chaplain's rage just grows stronger for the provocation. If Lemartes suffers an unsaved wound, but is not slain, his Strength and Attacks both immediately increase to 5.

DEATH COMPANY

In order to keep the Black Rage in check, on the eve of battle the Blood Angels bend their thoughts to prayer and to the sacrifice of their Primarch so many centuries ago. Chaplains move from man to man, blessing each in turn and noting those amongst the brotherhood whose eyes may appear a little glazed, or whose speech is slurred or overly excited. Some, almost all, overcome this ancient intrusion into their minds. Much of these warriors' training is directed at controlling it, beating it down into the depths of their being. But for some the imprint of Sanguinius is too strong, the memories too loud and demanding. As the Chaplains chant the moripatris – the mass of doom – the chosen ones collapse into the arms of their priests, and are taken away to form a special unit called the Death Company.

The warriors of the Death Company seek only one thing – death in battle – and they are sent forth to their final fight with great honour. Each brother is arrayed in black armour, blazoned with blood-red saltires to symbolise the wounds of Sanguinius during his final battle against Horus, and hung with scrolls that proclaim deeds performed and honours earned before the onset of madness. From the moment a Battle Brother dons the sepulchral armour of the Death Company he is a dead man walking, lost forever to his Chapter, but to be remembered eternally in its histories.

Members of the Death Company fight completely without fear, as befits warriors certain of their own demise, and the furious willpower lent them by the Black Rage renders them impervious to wounds that days before would have killed them outright. Under the watchful eyes of the Chapter's Chaplains, the Lost Brothers of the Death Company know glory beyond even the ken of their Battle-Brothers, fighting against terrible odds in one final service to their Chapter. Many of the Blood Angels' greatest victories have followed a shattering assault by the Death Company. There are few enemies who can hope to stay the onset of such maddened warriors, let alone repel their assault. On Antax, Mel'yanneth, Hollonan, Armageddon and other worlds too numerous to mention, the Death Company have more than lived up to their name, and legends of their ferocity have long since spread to worlds where the Blood Angels have never trod.

Yet as with all such glories, a price must be paid – either on the bloody ground of the battlefield, or in the fleeting calm of victory. Those few members of the Death Company that survive the battle perish shortly afterwards, either of their fearsome wounds or through the mercy of the Redeemer of the Lost, whose duty it is to end their suffering. It is better this way, for those who do survive almost always fall victim to the Red Thirst, turning into creatures no better than wild beasts craving flesh and blood. Better by far to die cleanly and quickly than to suffer such ignoble fate...

	WS	BS	S	T	W	I	A	Ld	Sv
Death Company	5	4	4	4	1	4	2	8	3+

UNIT TYPE: Infantry.

WARGEAR: Power armour, chainsword, boltgun or bolt pistol, frag and krak grenades.

SPECIAL RULES: Fearless, Feel No Pain, Furious Charge, Relentless.

Black Rage: The Death Company are subject to the Rage universal special rule. Furthermore, the Death Company never count as a scoring unit.

"Treat them with honour, my Brothers.
Not because they will bring us victory this day,
but because their fate will one day be ours."

– Astorath the Grim, Blood Angels High Chaplain

ASTORATH THE GRIM

Astorath the Grim is the Blood Angels' High Chaplain and Redeemer of the Lost. There is no rank within the Chapter more greatly honoured, or more deeply loathed. Honoured, for the burden the Redeemer of the Lost bears, and for the essential duty he performs; loathed because that duty is stained forever with the blood of his Battle-Brothers.

It is Astorath's calling to seek out those amongst the Scions of Sanguinius whose souls have been claimed by the Black Rage, and whose mental degeneration has become so severe that even death in battle is no longer possible. His quarry found, Astorath ends his Lost Brother's life with a single mighty blow to the neck, severing his head to thwart the fiendish endurance granted by the Black Rage. This is without doubt an act of mercy, a gift to the accursed. Nonetheless, no Battle-Brother can ever feel entirely comfortable in Astorath's presence, for they know that the bite of his forbidding axe might one day be the last thing that they feel.

Whilst officially bound to the Blood Angels, Astorath's duties carry him far and wide amongst the Chapter's successors. It was long ago considered that these terrible duties were best borne by a single brother and, thus far at least, a single brother has been equal to the task at hand. So does Astorath tread the stars, seeking those who require his blessing of oblivion.

To an observer, it might perhaps seem that Astorath's presence fans the destructive fires of the Black Rage. Certainly it is more prevalent wherever he treads, and even those Blood Angels who are yet sane are unmistakably wilder in the Redeemer's presence. However, the truth is entirely opposite.

Astorath can sense the Black Rage's degenerative onset before it becomes apparent to any other soul – including its victim. Individual afflictions echo through his mind in the form of doom-laden chords, and grow ever stronger as other Battle-Brothers fall into the Black Rage's clutches. No separation of distance can serve to mute this dolorous symphony. Be the victims fighting on Armageddon or in Ultramar, Astorath can sense their plight – and he must go to them as his duty requires.

So it is that the Redeemer of the Lost has become a true Angel of Death, a legend of destruction amongst the Blood Angels' successors and their foes alike. Wherever Astorath the Grim treads, the enemy face not only his fury, but the onslaught of Space Marines caught in the twilight shadows of the Black Rage. Astorath's sorrow for his doomed Battle-Brothers serves only to fuel a determination that they shall pass into death having known one last great victory. In this cause he fights like a man possessed, resolute that his twin gifts of death and redemption shall not be denied.

UNIT TYPE: Jump Infantry.

WARGEAR: Artificer armour, bolt pistol, frag and krak grenades, jump pack, Rosarius (see page 42).

The Executioner's Axe: The Executioner's Axe is a two-handed power weapon that strikes at Strength 6. Successful invulnerable saves taken against wounds caused by the Executioner's Axe must be re-rolled.

SPECIAL RULES: Descent of Angels, Independent Character.

Honour of the Chapter: Astorath utterly embodies the honour of Sanguinius, and the Blood Angels Chapter as a whole. He, and all members of a squad he has joined, are fearless, as described in the Warhammer 40,000 rulebook.

Liturgies of Blood: On a player turn in which he assaults, Astorath and all members of any squad he has joined can re-roll failed rolls to hit. Death Company models can also re-roll failed rolls to wound (their rage makes them particularly susceptible to Astorath's fiery oratory).

Shadow of the Primarch: If Astorath is included in the army, all Blood Angels units (friend and foe!) that have the Red Thirst special rule will succumb to its effects on a roll of 3 or less, rather than a roll of 1.

	WS	BS	S	T	W	I	A	Ld	Sv
Astorath the Grim	6	5	4	4	3	5	3	10	2+

LIBRARIANS

Blood Angels Librarians are the ultimate warrior mystics, set apart from their Battle-Brothers by their ability to harness incredible psychic energies. Few Blood Angels can become Librarians, for the psychic talent is a mutation of sorts and, though more common in the Blood Angels than in other Space Marine Chapters, it remains incredibly rare amongst the Chapter's recruits. Only by careful screening can potential new Librarians be identified, as it is crucial that they are pure of mind. Untrained human psykers are considered one of the greatest threats to the Imperium, and an unschooled psyker with all the hardiness, training and resolve of a Space Marine would surely be a thousand times deadlier.

It is to guard against such potential misuses of the Librarian's gift that his lessons must be as unforgiving as they are. Indeed, a Librarian's tutelage is far harsher and rigorous than that of an ordinary Blood Angel's. His magnificent mind must be armoured and strengthened to resist the seductive and empty promises of the Chaos Gods, whose insidious whispers are ever-present in a psyker's thoughts.

Yet alongside this training, the Librarian must still endure the same trials and challenges as his Battle-Brothers – sharpening his skill with bolter and blade, hardening his body to physical injury even as he guards his mind against doubt and fear. He is, after all, still a Space Marine, and must stand on equal footing with his comrades in times of war.

Gruelling though they may be, the Librarian's training serves well to transform him from a mere Battle-Brother to a fully-fledged weapon of psychic destruction. When in full control of his mind and abilities, a Librarian can cause blood to boil in its veins, shatter adamantium plates with blistering bolts of force or choke a foe's mind with an impenetrable cloud of fear. There are few limits on what a Librarian can achieve once he has fixed upon a goal, and less that the enemy can do to prevent his wrath.

Though they are welcomed and embraced as comrades by other Blood Angels, Librarians always stand somewhat apart from the rest of the Chapter. No bond of blood or battle can ever quite dispel the unease with which ordinary Blood Angels view their psychically-gifted brethren, for how can a non-psyker ever be truly comfortable with a Battle-Brother who can perform such violent miracles? Nor is there complete trust even within the ranks of the Librarians themselves, for they must keep watch over their fellows, so that should one fall to the whispered madness of Chaos or the Black Rage he can be slain, swiftly and mercifully, before he wreaks untold harm upon the Chapter that he once loyally served.

	WS	BS	S	T	W	I	A	Ld	Sv
Librarian	5	4	4	4	2	4	2	10	3+

UNIT TYPE: Infantry.

WARGEAR: Power armour, boltgun or bolt pistol, frag and krak grenades, force weapon.

Psychic hood: Psychic hoods are embedded with arcane constructions of psychically attuned crystals that allow a Librarian to disperse the energy of an enemy psyker's power.

Declare that you'll use the psychic hood after an enemy model within 24" of the Librarian passes a Psychic test. If there are several Librarians in range, only one can attempt to nullify the psychic power – you must choose which. Each player then rolls a D6 and adds their model's Leadership value to the score.

If the Space Marine Librarian beats the opposing model's score then the psychic power is nullified and does not take effect that turn. If the opposing model's score is equal or higher, it can use its psychic power as normal. The psychic hood can be used once each time an enemy model uses a psychic power within range.

SPECIAL RULES: And They Shall Know No Fear, Independent Character.

Psyker: A Blood Angels Librarian is a psyker, as described in the Warhammer 40,000 rulebook, and has two psychic powers from the list given on page 63 (chosen when the army is picked). He can only use one power each player turn unless he has been upgraded to an Epistolary, in which case he can use up to two psychic powers each turn.

A Smith

MEPHISTON, LORD OF DEATH

Mephiston was once Brother Calistarius, a Librarian of exceptional valour and strength of character. Yet the Black Rage cares not for the nobility of the soul, nor the deeds of the flesh. While Calistarius fought before the walls of Hades Hive, during the Second War for Armaggedon, the curse of Sanguinius stole upon him. Inducted into the Death Company, Calistarius took part in the final assault on the Ecclesorium building, and was one of the many crushed when the building collapsed in a shower of debris.

For seven days and seven nights Calistarius lay entombed, his fevered mind teetering on the edge of madness and his broken body on the verge of death. Yet Calistarius did not succumb. Through sheer force of will he confronted the uncontrollable rage that burned through his mangled form. With supreme effort, Calistarius cast out the Black Rage and, in so doing, became something far more than he had been before. At midnight on the seventh day he burst free from his rocky prison, reborn as Mephiston, Lord of Death.

His resurrection did not go unwitnessed. By this time Hades lay once more in the hands of the Imperium, but Orks still roamed the ruins. As Mephiston heaved ferrocrete boulders aside from his tomb, the sound of tortured stone drew the attention of one such band. Weaponless, and with his armour shredded and mangled, Mephiston must have seemed easy prey, but nothing could have been further from the truth. His gene-seed, dormant these many long years, had awakened and wrought further changes, granting exceptional strength and vigour. Moving with a speed the Orks could not match, Mephiston unleashed a flurry of attacks, every blow pulverising flesh and shattering bone. Five Orks died in as many seconds, and a dozen more swiftly followed. The greenskins never stood a chance, but they were as stubborn as Mephiston was determined. It was not until the reborn angel punched clean through the biggest Ork's chest and tore out his heart that the survivors fled. His ruined armour slick with the blood of his foes, Mephiston began the long walk to the Imperial lines.

Since that day, Mephiston has risen swiftly through the ranks of the Blood Angels and now holds the office of Chief Librarian. He is a figure of awe and reverence to most of his Battle-Brothers, who perceive him as a saviour in these times of woe. Others are not so accepting, for they have difficulty recognising the Calistarius of old in Mephiston. Calistarius was voluble, yet Mephiston's tongue is silent save at times of great need. Calistarius sought the company of his brothers both on and off the battlefield, yet Mephiston spends silent hours alone in thought, and his face, though noble beyond compare, somehow speaks of a soul still ill at ease. Perhaps these changes were inevitable, given the trial of transformation.

Yet there are whispers that Mephiston paid a dreadful price for his resurrection, that when he mastered the Black Rage something altogether more terrible took its place. It is to be hoped that such rumours are baseless, mere carrion latching onto greatness, but Mephiston keeps his secrets close, and only time will reveal the truth…

	WS	BS	S	T	W	I	A	Ld	Sv
Mephiston	7	5	6	6	5	7	4	10	2+

UNIT TYPE: Infantry.

WARGEAR: Artificer armour, plasma pistol, frag and krak grenades, force sword, psychic hood (see opposite).

SPECIAL RULES: And They Shall Know No Fear, Fleet.

Psyker: Mephiston knows the Sanguine Sword, Unleash Rage and Wings of Sanguinius Psychic powers (see page 63). He can use three Psychic powers each turn.

Transfixing Gaze: At the start of the Assault phase, Mephiston can attempt to enthrall a single enemy independent character in base contact. Once selected, the target immediately takes a Leadership test with a -4 modifier (a double 1 always passes). If the test is passed, there is no ill effect. If the test is failed, Mephiston re-rolls all failed attempts to hit and to wound against the enthralled target for the duration of that Assault phase (note that being enthralled does not prevent the target from attacking – providing he survives long enough, of course).

SANGUINARY PRIESTS

Every Space Marine Legion, and every Chapter that has followed in those hallowed footsteps, has maintained a corps of Apothecaries to safeguard its gene-seed and the health of its Battle-Brothers. Yet Sanguinius knew that his Battle-Brothers would require more than physical curatives if they were to endure the endless war that was to be their mission in the years to come. The Blood Angels Primarch foresaw the shadow of death that would come to nestle in his scions' hearts – though he knew not how it would descend – and judged that constant guidance would be needed to put this darkness to proper use. So did he transform the Legion's Apothecaries into Sanguinary Priests, setting them as high in honour as the Chaplains of the Reclusiam, and as vital to the spiritual guidance of the Blood Angels.

Whilst the sermons and ceremonies of the Chapter's Chaplains exhort their Battle-Brothers to reject the anger within, those performed by the Sanguinary Priests call upon the Blood Angels to embrace the Red Thirst and wrest it to their control; unleashing its strength to buttress theirs when the day is darkest and the battle goes ill. Even to this day, the Sanguine Tower of the Priesthood is the only part of the fortress monastery that challenges the dark glory of the Chapter's Reclusiam. These two towers – one a shining beacon of redemption and renewal, the other sinister and sombre – remain a physical monument to the dual nature at the heart of every Blood Angels' soul.

As with the Apothecaries of other Chapters, the foremost concern of the Sanguinary Priests is to conserve the Chapter's gene-seed. If a wounded Blood Angel can be saved from the clutches of death, the Sanguinary Priest will do his utmost to preserve his Battle Brother's life, tending wounds and applying restorative salves whose closely-guarded secrets remain unknown outside the alabaster walls of the Sanguine Tower. As the injured Blood Angel is returned to full fighting health, so will the gene-seed within him survive and the Chapter endure.

Yet there are weapons in the galaxy that can overcome even the legendary constitution of a Space Marine, and even lesser tools will serve to render a Blood Angel incapable of recovery should enough blows find their mark. In such cases, the Sanguinary Priest can do little but calm the spirit of his dying Battle Brother in preparation for oblivion, sometimes relieving his charge's mortal agonies with a single shot. Once death has come, the Sanguinary Priest performs one final act for his fallen comrade, extracting the progenoid organs – the reservoirs of gene-seed – from the corpse. This is by far the hardest part of a Sanguinary Priest's duties, for the Red Thirst cares little for the nature of blood – only that it is warm and flowing. So it is that every gene-seed extraction performed by a Sanguinary Priest becomes not only a ritual necessary for the continuation of the Chapter, but also a trial for the mind and soul of the Sanguinary Priest himself.

	WS	BS	S	T	W	I	A	Ld	Sv
Sanguinary Priest	5	4	4	4	1	4	2	9	3+

UNIT TYPE: Infantry.

WARGEAR: Power armour, chainsword, bolt pistol, frag and krak grenades.

Blood Chalice: All friendly units within 6" are subject to the Furious Charge and Feel No Pain special rules.

SPECIAL RULES: And They Shall Know No Fear, Independent Character.

BLOOD CHALICE

The very first Blood Chalices were presented to the priesthood by Sanguinius himself. Legend has it that the Primarch somehow placed a part of his being into each vessel, and that the bearer of the relic and all Battle-Brothers nearby can hear Sanguinius' voice in their mind, urging them to greater glories.

Over the long centuries, many Blood Chalices have been lost to the caprices of war and, though there are no longer Blood Chalices equal to the number of priests, each narcethium – the Sanguinary Priest's chief tool of healing – contains a shard from a shattered Blood Chalice so that the blessing is not lost.

BROTHER CORBULO

Corbulo is the Sanguinary High Priest of the Blood Angels, keeper of the initiation mysteries and guardian of the Red Grail. It is said that no other Blood Angel resembles Sanguinius as closely does Corbulo, whose piercing eyes and noble aspect reflect the nature of the Blood Angels at its most pure. It is perhaps this perfection that has driven Corbulo to such lengths in search of a cure for the Red Thirst. In the centuries since his investiture, Corbulo has worked ceaselessly to isolate and neutralise the Flaw in the Blood Angels' gene-seed. This quest has taken him all over the galaxy, from other Space Marine Chapters in order to learn from their Apothecaries, to forgotten worlds in search of forbidden archeotech from the Dark Age of Technology.

Corbulo's resemblance to the fallen Primarch is not merely physical. His deep wisdom and canny insights are legendary, and his counsel has proven invaluable time and again. More tellingly, Corbulo shares Sanguinius' gift of the far-seeing eye, and can discern the patterns and shapes of a future yet to come – a gift that has manifested only sparingly through the many generations of Blood Angels. Those scant hours not claimed by duty or in search of the Red Thirst's cure, Corbulo spends poring over the Scrolls of Sanguinius, seeking to combine knowledge from the Primarch's visions with the fleeting insights distilled from his own.

Corbulo's travails in this regard have borne fruit many times. That the Blood Angels arrived so swiftly on Armageddon following Ghazghkull's initial invasion – and at Chapter strength – was due in part to Corbulo's divinations. Similarly, without Corbulo's guidance, the Blood Angel's Chapter Fleet would never have known the hour and location at which M'kar the Reborn's world-breaking Daemon-cruiser would enter the Baal system, and could thus never have ambushed and obliterated the vessel before Baal itself was laid waste. Yet these successful predictions have not been without cost. In recent years, Corbulo has grown ever more withdrawn and taciturn, and his eyes have taken on a haunted look that he cannot easily conceal. Though the exact detail of what Corbulo has learnt remains a closely-guarded secret, it cannot be doubted that the very blackest of times lie ahead for the Blood Angels – events so dire that even foreknowledge is of no protection.

THE RED GRAIL

As Sanguinary High Priest, Corbulo is charged with the wardenship of the Red Grail, the very chalice in which the blood of Sanguinius was preserved after the Primarch's death. This vessel is a key part of the induction mysteries of the Sanguinary Priests, but it is also a potent relic upon the field of battle.

Blood Angels in the presence of the Red Grail find themselves reinvigorated, the physical and psychological aspects inherited from their Primarch enhanced in some unknowable way. Impossible though it may seem, perhaps some residual trace of Sanguinius' spirit lingers within the grail, exhorting his scions to greater deeds…

	WS	BS	S	T	W	I	A	Ld	Sv
Corbulo	5	5	4	4	2	5	3	9	3+

UNIT TYPE: Infantry.

WARGEAR: Power armour, bolt pistol, frag and krak grenades.

Heaven's Teeth: This chainsword is a treasured and irreplaceable relic from the time of Sanguinius. Corbulo's close combat attacks are made at Strength 5 and have the Rending special rule.

The Red Grail: All friendly units within 6" of Corbulo are subject to the Furious Charge and Feel No Pain special rules. Any Feel No Pain roll taken for Corbulo himself is passed on a 2+, rather than a 4+.

SPECIAL RULES: And They Shall Know No Fear, Independent Character.

The Far-Seeing Eye: Corbulo allows you a single re-roll once per game. This can be any roll you have made, such as for an armour save, a Leadership test, a To Hit roll, a scatter roll or even to seize the Initiative. If Corbulo is slain before this re-roll is used, then it is lost.

SANGUINARY GUARD

The Sanguinary Guard are the uttermost elite of the Blood Angels, proven in mind, body and spirit to uphold the values of their illustrious Primarch to an extent that no other can.

The very first Sanguinary Guard were the bodyguard of the Primarch himself throughout the days of the Great Crusade. They fought alongside Sanguinius through the terrible battles on Dalos, Blindhope, Signus Prime and countless others, ultimately perishing in the assault on Horus' Battle Barge that claimed their Primarch's life. Only one member of the Sanguinary Guard survived that final battle. Sanguinius' foreboding of his own fate led him to insist that his Herald, Azkaellon, remain on Terra so that should the worst befall, the Sanguinary Guard would not be extinguished, and could be reconstituted to serve as a beacon of hope in the dark days ahead. With heavy heart, Azkaellon acceded to the Primarch's wishes, for though he yearned to fight at Sanguinius' side one last time, he could not jeopardise the duty entrusted to him. So it was that the Sanguinary Guard survived where their Primarch did not, for Azkaellon made certain that their legacy was maintained, not just in the Blood Angels, but in every Successor Chapter that arose from the dissolution of the mighty Blood Angels Legion.

Unlike the Chapter's other veterans, the Sanguinary Guards do not select wargear according to their expertise. Instead they fight with the weapons traditional to their position –

wrist-mounted Angelus boltguns that leave both hands free for the wielding of crackling power glaives. Each guardian's golden armour is a relic of the Chapter, one of a handful of surviving suits from the times of the Great Crusade, whose secrets of manufacture have long since been lost. There are few more revered relics in the whole of the Chapter's armoury, for they are a tangible reminder of the very greatest days of not only the Blood Angels, but of the Imperium as a whole.

The deeds of each Sanguinary Guard are recorded with reverent diligence. At high feast days, those rare occasions when the entire Chapter is gathered together, the Sanguinary Guard's deeds are recounted, delivered with gusto and pride by battle-steeped veterans to attentive Scouts and aspirants. They speak of Blind Erephon, who claimed he fought better without his eyes than he ever did with them, and who sealed the seven Daemon-gates of Derios IV. Of Andrastor, who stood alone against the Tyranid swarm on Cripple Ridge. Of Saronath, whose coming was so terrible it set Waaagh! Rokchewa to flight, and of Sepharan, who entered the gates of hell itself to battle for his Chapter's soul. Of these warriors they tell, and of countless others, past and present. To join the ranks of the Sanguinary Guard is therefore no mere battlefield assignment, nor even an honour. Rather it is to enter a brotherhood of mortals-become-gods, to continue a legend ten thousand years old.

	WS	BS	S	T	W	I	A	Ld	Sv
Sanguinary Guard	4	4	4	4	1	4	2	10	2+

UNIT TYPE: Jump Infantry.

WARGEAR: Artificer armour, jump pack, frag and krak grenades.

Glaive Encarmine: A Glaive Encarmine is a two-handed master-crafted power weapon.

Angelus Boltgun: The Angelus boltgun is a variation on the ubiquitous Space Marine weapon, used exclusively by the Blood Angels and their successors. Its magazine is loaded with very rare and potent bloodshard shells, whose razor-filament payloads make a mockery of most armour.

Range	Strength	AP	Type
12"	4	4	Assault 2

Chapter Banner: See page 52 for details.

Death Mask: Golden energy dances across the Death Mask to form a horrifying halo. An enemy assaulted by one or more unit equipped with Death Masks must pass a Leadership test or be reduced to Weapon Skill 1 for the duration of the Assault phase.

SPECIAL RULES: Descent of Angels, The Red Thirst, Fearless.

THE SANGUINOR

The Sanguinor is a golden angel of vengeance who descends from the heavens only in times of the Blood Angels' greatest need. To most he is a myth, an honoured part of the Chapter's traditions and mysteries. After all, so dire are the circumstances in which the Sanguinor appears that few behold his glory and survive to speak of it. Only those who have access to the records laid down in the Chapter's Reclusiam are certain that the Sanguinor is no mere legend or hallucination. There, in the pages of a single iron-clasped volume, are recorded the accounts of the Sanguinor's manifestations across the millennia. Yet most famous of all, and most readily recounted, is the legend of the assault upon the Night Lords' Battle Barge *Terrorclaw*.

So it was that twelve Battle-Brothers were ordered to strike at the *Terrorclaw*, to slay its master as penance for unrecorded transgressions. No one expected them to succeed, for they were outnumbered several hundred times over, yet the Sanguinor seemingly saw merit in their task and joined the fight at the moment their boarding torpedo crashed through the Battle Barge's hull. Pausing only to grant his blessing to the sergeant in command of the sortie, he cut a bloody path through the *Terrorclaw*'s defenders, blazing through the vessel like a hot and angry wind.

Tellingly, the Sanguinor's actions that day did not grant his penitent Battle-Brothers an easy victory. Though their passage to the command deck was made upon the carpet of dismembered bodies and severed limbs left in the Sanguinor's wake, the Blood Angels had to fight every step of the way against a crew of Chaos Space Marines, themselves hungry for vengeance. Though the quest was ultimately a success and the Captain of the *Terrorclaw* slain, only the sergeant survived and returned to Baal. The Sanguinor did therefore not accomplish the quest for his Battle-Brothers, but through his might and wrath he did render the impossible possible. The name of the sergeant has been lost from the records concerning the *Terrorclaw*, but Dante occasionally casts his mind back to those times, and with a slight smile recalls the sergeant's renewed faith in his own skills, and of his Chapter's mission.

Yet it is one thing to know the Sanguinor's deeds, quite another to determine his nature. A few amongst the Chapter Council argue that he is the coalescion of the Primarch's nobler side, the part that kept Sanguinius' darkness in check, and that was lost to the Blood Angels upon his death. The Sanguinary Guard believe him irrefutably to be none other than Azkaellon, founder of their order, preserved against the withering millennia by the Emperor's grace. So great is the Sanguinor's legend that it has long ago passed beyond the Blood Angels Chapter, and has served to exacerbate the discomfort felt towards the Blood Angels by certain sections of the Imperium. The Inquisition in particular worry that the Sanguinor is some form of psychic construct, and that his existence proves the Blood Angels to be just as flawed spiritually as they are physically. Yet for all the vexation the Sanguinor might cause outsiders, to his Battle-Brothers he is an honoured part of their heritage, no more needing of query than the blood that flows through their veins.

	WS	BS	S	T	W	I	A	Ld	Sv
The Sanguinor	8	5	5	4	3	6	5	10	2+

UNIT TYPE: Jump Infantry.

WARGEAR: Artificer armour, frag and krak grenades, jump pack, Glaive Encarmine (see opposite).

SPECIAL RULES: Descent of Angels, Eternal Warrior, Fearless, Furious Charge.

Avenging Angel: As soon as the Sanguinor is placed onto the table, choose one of your opponent's HQ units. The Sanguinor re-rolls all failed To Hit and To Wound rolls against the chosen unit for the remainder of the battle.

The Sanguinor's Blessing: When your force is deployed, randomly choose one Sergeant in your army to receive the sacred blessing of the Sanguinor – that model has +1 Weapon Skill, +1 Wound, +1 Initiative and +1 Attack for the remainder of the battle.

Unyielding Will: The Sanguinor has a 3+ invulnerable save

Aura of Fervour: All friendly units within 6" of the Sanguinor (except for the Sanguinor himself) have +1 Attack.

HONOUR GUARD

A high-ranking Blood Angels officer is often accompanied to battle by a dedicated squad of bodyguards known as an Honour Guard. The tactical and strategic knowledge of an experienced Chapter Master or Captain is perhaps the most deadly of all the weapons wielded by a Blood Angels' strike force, and is worthy therefore of the greatest protection his Chapter can provide.

Honour Guards are chosen only from a company's most experienced warriors. Indeed many are veterans seconded from the Chapter's famous 1st Company. Each Honour Guard is therefore a canny and deadly warrior in his own right. He will need to be – an Honour Guard's charge is ever to be found in the very heart of the fighting and, where he goes, they are duty bound to follow. Naturally, an Honour Guardian's years of service will have sharpened more than his combat skills. Some will have seen more battles than the Captain they accompany, and possess a wealth of tactical insights. It is not unusual therefore for an Honour Guard to form the core of a Captain's inner sanctum of advisors, lending their accumulated wisdom and experience to his weighty decisions.

The specific armament and specialities of an Honour Guard's members can vary greatly according to the temperament and tactical preference of their officer. A commander who prefers to spearhead his strike force's attacks might well choose

seasoned Assault Marines to form his bodyguard, or Battle-Brothers practiced with close-range special weapons, such as flamers or plasma guns. Such a deployment is perilous in the extreme, and a commander who chooses this path will take care not to risk any of the Chapter relics. Older and wiser officers instead select their Honour Guards to help create a visible anchor-point on the battlefield. Such officers go to war accompanied by the Company's Standard Bearer and Champion, forming an easily identifiable and adaptable rally point around which the battle inevitably focuses. A particularly respected officer can even call upon one of the Chapter's novitiate Sanguinary Priests to serve in his Honour Guard and bestow the benediction of his Blood Chalice upon the squad and all other Blood Angels who fight alongside him.

Much prestige and distinction is bestowed upon those called to service in an Honour Guard, but such duty is incredibly perilous. Nonetheless, it is almost unheard of for a commission to its ranks to be refused. Blood Angels, like all Space Marines, hold their honour, and that of the Chapter, far higher than their mortal existence. Furthermore, there is no finer opportunity for a Blood Angel to prove his worth to the Chapter and the Emperor than by service in an Honour Guard. Should an Honour Guardian survive his duties then promotion will surely follow, perhaps to the 1st Company, but possibly even to a captaincy of his own.

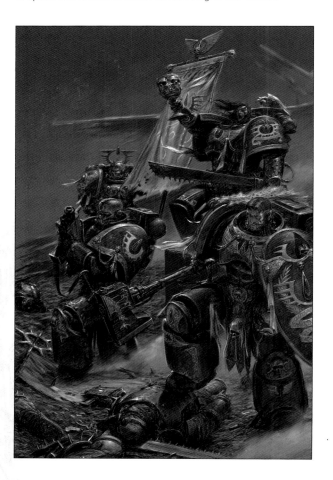

	WS	BS	S	T	W	I	A	Ld	Sv
Honour Guard	4	4	4	4	1	4	2	9	3+
Blood Champion	5	4	4	4	1	4	2	9	3+
Sanguinary Novitiate	4	4	4	4	1	4	2	9	3+

UNIT TYPE: Infantry.

WARGEAR: Power armour, boltgun or bolt pistol, chainsword, frag and krak grenades.

Blood Chalice: All friendly units within 6" of the Sanguinary Novitiate are subject to the Furious Charge and Feel No Pain special rules.

Chapter Banner: All friendly units within 12" of the banner bearer re-roll failed Morale and Pinning Tests. In addition, all models in the same unit as the Chapter Banner have +1 Attack whilst the banner bearer is alive.

Company Standard: All friendly units within 12" of the standard bearer re-rolls failed Morale and Pinning tests. In addition, while the standard bearer is still alive, the Honour Guard counts as scoring one extra wound in close combat for the purposes of calculating the assault result.

SPECIAL RULES: And They Shall Know No Fear, The Red Thirst.

COMMANDER DANTE

As the Imperium enters the Time of Ending, the Blood Angels are ruled over by Commander Dante, Lord of the Host and Bringer of Sanguinius' Light. Dante is truly a legend, for his deeds span many long centuries. Indeed, he is thought by many to be the oldest living Space Marine. Even Captain Lysander of the Imperial Fists, who was lost in the eddies and tides of Warpspace for a thousand years, cannot recall a time when Dante did not reign supreme over the Blood Angels.

None can deny the scope of Dante's campaign experience. He has fought battles uncounted, orchestrated innumerable major campaigns and seized bloody victory on worlds as far-flung as Ultima Macharia and star-swept Jonol. It is said that no man has visited as many of the Imperium's million worlds as Dante, and he has come to each in full raiment of war, at the head of a glorious and vengeful host.

To his fellow Chapter Masters, Dante is an exemplar of the fearlessness, dedication and strategic genius that speak to the heart of the Space Marines' never-ending mission. To the hard-pressed generals and marshals of the Imperial Guard he is a thrice-welcomed and honoured ally in the forefront of Mankind's defence. To the common soldiers and citizens of the Imperium, Dante is nothing less than a saviour, a golden god who descends from the heavens on wings of fire.

So long now has Dante lived that his exploits have passed into myth. It is now impossible to say how many Ork heads Dante cleaved at the Liberation of Canau, for the tally grows greater each time the story is recounted. Did Dante truly defeat the Bloodthirster Skarbrand before the Gates of Pandemonium? Was it indeed a single mighty blow that clove the Daemon in twain? Only Dante himself can say with certainty. Yet he speaks not on such events, no matter how much the exaggerated nature of such tales must rankle with his warrior pride. The Imperium needs heroes – needs hope – in these dark times, and the Commander of the Blood Angels keeps his peace so that Mankind does not lose heart.

Yet for all his success, or perhaps because of it, Dante has grown weary of his burdens. He has lived far longer than he should, and the burden of centuries grows ever weightier. Only one thing prevents Dante succumbing to ennui. Recorded in the Scrolls of Sanguinius are the Primarch's visions of a great battle to overshadow all others, where one golden warrior will stand between his Emperor and the darkness. For many generations of the Blood Angels, these prophecies have been read as Sanguinius' foreknowledge of his own fate, yet through some instinct, perhaps a lingering trace of his Primarch's fabled far-seeing eye, Dante believes otherwise. One day, perhaps one day soon, the defence of the Emperor will rest in Dante's hands, and he aims to fulfil this final duty.

	WS	BS	S	T	W	I	A	Ld	Sv
Commander Dante	6	5	4	4	4	6	4	10	2+

UNIT TYPE: Jump Infantry.

WARGEAR: Artificer armour, infernus pistol, jump pack, frag and krak grenades, Iron Halo (see page 40).

Death Mask of Sanguinius: This ancient artefact resonates with the Primarch's rage at Horus' treachery, and can be used to call down a curse upon a foe.

Before forces are deployed, choose one enemy independent character: that model has -1 Weapon Skill, -1 Wound, -1 Initiative and -1 Attack (all to a minimum of 1) for the remainder of the battle. The Death Mask of Sanguinius otherwise follows the rules for Death Masks given in the Sanguinary Guard entry on page 50.

The Axe Mortalis: The Axe Mortalis is a master-crafted power weapon.

SPECIAL RULES: And They Shall Know No Fear, Descent of Angels, Independent Character.

Tactical Precision: Commander Dante (and his unit, if he has joined one and they have jump packs) does not scatter when it deploys by Deep Strike.

Surgical Strike: Commander Dante (and any squad he has joined) have the Hit and Run universal special rule.

BLOOD ANGELS SUCCESSORS

Though they have never been so prolific as the Ultramarines or Imperial Fists, the Blood Angels are not without their Successor Chapters. Most were founded in the days following the Horus Heresy, before the grim truth concerning their flawed gene-seed came to light. These Chapters are strongly bound to the Blood Angels, united by blood and tradition in a way difficult for outsiders to understand. To attack one is to invite the wrath of all, for whatever differences and rivalries might exist between these Chapters, they are all the Scions of Sanguinius, whose loyalty to the Primarch's memory transcends all other duties and concerns.

Born as they were from the Blood Angels' gene-seed, every Successor Chapter carries the Flaw, although some feel its taint more than others. Most harshly affected are those successors founded in later centuries, at times when the Blood Angels Chapter Council had thought the Flaw eradicated from the gene-stocks. In reality, it had merely degenerated into new and worrying forms and, as a result, the Battle Brothers of those Chapters founded in such times do not suffer slight lapses of control, but teeter on the border of full-blown insanity.

The Chapters described here are the most famous of the Blood Angels' successors, but this list is by no means complete. Others have come and gone in the millennia since the dissolution of the Blood Angels Legion. Some, such as the Knights Sanguine, were consumed by war. Others, most famously the Exsanguinators and the Flesh Eaters, were fatally undone by their gene-seed. There are other surviving Chapters whose names and traditions would suggest a connection with the Blood Angels – the Blood Swords and Blood Ravens amongst them – but these Chapters do not claim Sanguinius' lineage, truthfully or otherwise.

Flesh Tearers   Second Founding
The Flesh Tearers' blood-rage is infamous across the Imperium, as are the deeds purported to have been performed by the Chapter's Battle-Brothers upon the battlefield. So divorced have the Flesh Tearers become from the rest of Mankind that most Imperial Commanders embrace the Chapter's offers of assistance only in the direst need. This unsavoury reputation has only been exacerbated by rumours of blood rituals in the wake of particularly successful campaigns.

Angels Vermillion   Second Founding
Alone of the Blood Angels' successors, the Angels Vermillion shun all contact with their Brother Chapters, choosing to bear their lingering curse in solitude and isolation. Little is recorded of the Angels Vermillions' actions in the days since the Second Founding, but whenever the Chapter is mentioned, its battle record is nothing short of exemplary. It is impossible to say why the Chapter has chosen to endure its curse without the support of its brothers – perhaps they feel the shame must be borne alone, or perhaps they have darker cause...

Blood Drinkers   Unknown Founding
Rather than deny the blood-lust that echoes through their souls, the Blood Drinkers have embraced it, making it a central part of their many rituals. In so doing, the Chapter seems to have achieved an unprecedented level of control over the Flaw, though it remains to be seen if this is but the first step on a long road to eventual damnation. Nevertheless, the Blood Drinkers ever aspire to be better than their corrupted flesh, striving endlessly to be judged as equals with the other Chapters of legend.

Angels Encarmine   Second Founding
It is said that no Space Marine Chapter is as active as the Angels Encarmine. Their Chapter Master, Castellan Zargo, cannot rest at peace and so forever seeks opportunities to lead his Battle Brothers on campaign. As a result, the Angels Encarmine are rarely at full strength, though what they lack in numbers is more than compensated for in determined fervour. It is worrying to note that the Angels Encarmine's Death Company rarely numbers less than thirty warriors, implying increasing instability in their gene-seed.

Angels Sanguine   Second Founding
The history of the Angels Sanguine is long and glorious, indeed the Chapter has been pivotal in many victories against the horrors emerging from the Eye of Terror. Yet the shadow of the Flaw lingers ever about the Angels Sanguine. What drives the Chapter's Battle Brothers to shield their faces from the gaze of others, never removing their helms save for in the privacy of their fortress monastery? And what is the secret of the catacombs that lie beneath the Chapter's home?

The Lamenters   Twenty-first Founding
The Lamenters have had a somewhat tumultuous history. The Chapter barely survived the repercussions of aligning themselves with Huron Blackheart's Astral Claws during the Badab War, and less than a century later was almost obliterated by Hive Fleet Kraken. Since then, the Lamenters have reportedly claimed the ability to cure their flawed gene-seed, though if anything the Chapter has undergone marked degeneration since their discovery, raising severe doubts as to the effectiveness of the 'cure'.

Knights of Blood   Unknown Founding
At the start of M41, following several centuries of the most terrible rage-fuelled carnage against enemies and allies alike, the Knights of Bloods were finally decreed Renegade by the High Lords of Terra. Nonetheless, they continued their galactic crusade, supposedly purging the Emperor's foes from the worlds of the Imperium. They are unwelcome allies at best, as any world that accepts their aid runs the risk of Inquisitorial investigation, in addition to the inherent dangers of fighting alongside the near-crazed Knights of Blood Battle-Brothers.

CHAPTER MASTER GABRIEL SETH

Gabriel Seth became Master of the Flesh Tearers as his Chapter stood upon the brink of annihilation. Millennia of unrelenting savagery had left the Chapter shunned and distrusted by many of the Imperium's fighting forces. Other Space Marine Chapters viewed the Flesh Tearers as being but a single step from turning renegade, and the Inquisition sought to have the Chapter investigated. Worse, mutation in the Flesh Tearers' gene-seed had exacerbated Sanguinius' curse, increasing the incidence of the Black Rage. Even those Flesh Tearers fortunate enough to escape the Black Rage were gripped by a bloodthirsty recklessness that inevitably cost many lives whenever the Chapter went to war.

On the day of his ascension, Seth listened grim-faced as the Chapter's Sanguinary Priests presented the evidence of the terrible truth – the rate at which their Battle-Brothers succumbed to madness or death now far exceeded the Flesh Tearers' capacity to replace their losses. Within two centuries, the Flesh Tearers would be no more, abandoned by their allies and betrayed by their own flesh. At that moment, Seth swore that if the Flesh Tearers' fate be extinction, then they would pass into history in proud remembrance, not through whispered rumours of brutality and madness.

Under Seth's leadership, the Flesh Tearers' Chapter Planet of Cretacia has become little more than an automated armoury and recruitment centre. At any given time, the bulk of the Flesh Tearers are off-planet, performing great patrol-arcs through the Segmentums Ultima and Tempestus, the Chapter's Librarians sifting the ether in search of astropathic calls for assistance. So it is that the Flesh Tearers will often be amongst the first wave of reinforcements to an embattled world, Seth himself leading boarding actions against enemy blockade vessels or counter-assaults on the invaders' drop zones before the foe have claimed so much as a foothold. Seth knows that he cannot realistically curtail his Battle-Brothers' bloodlust – indeed he himself is as prone to rage-soaked savagery as any of his brethren. Yet by striking first, and in isolation from other forces, the Flesh Tearers' worst excesses are concealed, as is the collateral damage amongst allies that once was the hallmark of the Chapter's assaults. Now, worlds that once reviled the Flesh Tearers praise them as saviours, and Seth as the bringer of that salvation.

It is too early to tell if Seth's strategy will ultimately bear fruit, if the Flesh Tearers can regain their place amongst the Imperium's pantheon of honoured defenders. Despite his intentions, Seth has done little to dispel the mistrust of his staunchest critics, in whom the memory of plans frustrated by the Flesh Tearers' impetuous assaults lies too fresh. Such things are of little concern to the Flesh Tearers Chapter Master, for, in his heart, Seth has never truly abandoned hope that the Flesh Tearers can be spared from ultimate oblivion. It is a desperate hope, at best. What fate ultimately lies in store for the Flesh Tearers and their Chapter Master, only time will tell...

UNIT TYPE: Infantry.

WARGEAR: Power armour, bolt pistol, frag and krak grenades, Iron Halo (see page 40).

Blood Reaver: Never was a weapon so aptly named as Seth's massive chainsword. Blood Reaver is a two-handed weapon. Hits from Blood Reaver are resolved at Strength 8 and have the Rending special rule.

SPECIAL RULES: Fearless, Independent Character.

Whirlwind of Gore: Instead of making his normal attacks, Seth can instead choose to whirl Blood Reaver in a glittering, gore-splattered arc. If he does so, Seth inflicts a single automatic hit on all enemy models in base contact. Declare whether or not Seth will perform a Whirlwind of Gore before any blows are struck.

Ferocious Instincts: Should an enemy drop its guard, Seth is swift to take advantage, lashing out with a swift punch, kick or headbutt to knock the foolhardy foe to the floor.

For every roll of '1' to hit Seth in close combat, enemy units immediately suffer an automatic Strength 4 hit as the Chapter Master takes advantage of the opening.

	WS	BS	S	T	W	I	A	Ld	Sv
Gabriel Seth	6	5	4	4	4	5	4	10	3+

WARGEAR

This section of Codex: Blood Angels lists the weapons and equipment used by the Blood Angels, along with the rules for using them in your games of Warhammer 40,000.

Weapons and equipment that can be used by more than one type of model or unit are detailed here, while equipment that is unique to a single model or unit (including wargear carried by named special characters) is often detailed in the appropriate entry in The Angelic Host section.

For example, bolters are ubiquitous and carried by many models, and so are detailed in this section. The Angelus boltgun, however, is unique to the Sanguinary Guard. While you will find a page reference here, the rules are detailed in the Sanguinary Guard entry.

WEAPONS

Assault Cannon

The rapidly rotating, multiple barrels of an assault cannon unleash a storm of shells, each one capable of shredding a man. The sheer volume of fire means that an assault cannon can be turned against infantry or even vehicles, where the overwhelming salvo of shells is capable of shredding even the heaviest armour.

Range	Strength	AP	Type
24"	6	4	Heavy 4, Rending

Astartes Grenade Launcher

These grenade launchers are loaded with frag and krak grenades and outfitted with adaptive targeting systems to compensate for the high speeds at which Scout Bikers commonly travel. Each time a grenade launcher fires, the controlling player chooses which type of ammo is used.

Frag Grenade

Range	Strength	AP	Type
24"	3	6	Rapid Fire, Blast

Krak Grenade

Range	Strength	AP	Type
24"	6	4	Rapid Fire

Boltgun

The boltgun, or bolter, fires small missiles, or 'bolts'. Each self-propelled bolt explodes with devastating effect once it has penetrated its target, blowing it apart from the inside.

Range	Strength	AP	Type
24"	4	5	Rapid Fire

Bolt Pistol

Bolt pistols are smaller versions of bolters. They are perfect side arms for Space Marines and are wielded alongside the chainsword by Assault Marines.

Range	Strength	AP	Type
12"	4	5	Pistol

Chainfist

A chainfist is a power fist fitted with a chainblade attachment designed to carve its way through armoured bulkheads or armour plating.

A chainfist is treated exactly as a power fist, but rolls an additional D6 for its armour penetration value.

Chainsword or Combat Blade

Space Marines utilise an array of close combat weapons, from the combat blades wielded by Scouts to the chainswords carried by Assault Marines. All are equally deadly in the hands of a Space Marine.

Both chainswords and combat blades are close combat weapons, as described in the Warhammer 40,000 rulebook.

Combi-Weapons

Combi-weapons are bolters that have been specially modified by the Chapter's most skilled artisans. Each has been expertly converted to house another weapon, either a meltagun, plasma gun or flamer. This extra weapon carries only a limited charge, allowing the bearer a single shot, perfect for emergencies and shots of opportunity.

A Space Marine armed with a combi-weapon (combi-meltagun, combi-plasma gun or combi-flamer) can choose to fire either the bolter, or the secondary weapon, each with the profile listed elsewhere in this section.

The bolter can be fired every turn, but the secondary weapon can only be fired once per battle (a combi-plasma gun can, of course, Rapid Fire). You cannot fire both weapons in the same turn.

Cyclone Missile Launcher

The cyclone is a specially designed missile launcher system, used by Space Marines in Terminator armour to provide mobile heavy fire support. Essentially a rack of missiles fitted onto the shoulders of a Terminator, the cyclone missile launcher enables the Terminator to engage both heavily armoured vehicles and lightly armoured infantry with deadly efficiency.

A Terminator can fire his cyclone missile launcher in addition to his storm bolter. Each time a cyclone missile launcher fires, the controlling player can choose which type of missile is being used.

Frag

Range	Strength	AP	Type
48"	4	6	Heavy 2, Blast

Krak

Range	Strength	AP	Type
48"	8	3	Heavy 2

Flamer

Flamers spew a highly volatile cloud of liquid chemicals that ignites on contact with air. Flamers are primarily used to scour the enemy from defended positions, their belches of superheated vapour slaughtering the foe in a fiery conflagration.

Range	Strength	AP	Type
Template	4	5	Assault 1

Frag Grenade

Frag grenades are explosive devices that are hurled at the enemy prior to an assault. The storm of shrapnel from the exploding frag grenades drives opponents further into cover for a few precious moments while the attackers close in.

Frag grenades are assault grenades, as described in the Warhammer 40,000 rulebook.

Hand Flamer

The hand flamer is a smaller version of the flamer. It is much prized by the Blood Angels as it is compact enough to allow a Battle-Brother to wield one alongside a chainsword.

Range	Strength	AP	Type
Template	3	6	Pistol

Heavy Bolter

An enormous version of the boltgun, the heavy bolter fires fist-sized bolts at the enemy with a staggering rate of fire.

Range	Strength	AP	Type
36"	5	4	Heavy 3

Heavy Flamer

The heavy flamer is the ultimate weapon for sweeping fortifications clear and purging the ranks of the enemy at close quarters.

Range	Strength	AP	Type
Template	5	4	Assault 1

Infernus Pistol

Blood Angels infernus pistols are amongst the Chapter's most prized relics, for they date back to the Dark Age of Technology. Each infernus pistol is essentially a pistol-sized meltagun whose fury can pierce the heaviest armour.

Range	Strength	AP	Type
6"	8	1	Pistol, Melta

Krak Grenade

Krak grenades are armour piercing bombs, designed to crack open the armoured hulls of enemy vehicles. Though they lack the explosive force of melta bombs or other specialised demolition charges, they are small and easy to carry, making them ideal weapons of opportunity.

See the Warhammer 40,000 rulebook for details of using krak grenades.

Lascannon

There are few finer weapons for tank hunting on the battlefields of the 41st Millenium than the lascannon. Within the gun is a laser chamber that charges an energy blast capable of shattering any enemy vehicle with a single shot. The lascannons used by Space Marine forces vary considerably, from the man-portable variants carried by Devastator squads, to the godhammer-pattern lascannons borne by the mighty Land Raider.

Range	Strength	AP	Type
48"	9	2	Heavy 1

Lightning Claw

Lightning claws are heavily armoured gauntlets with long, slashing talons sheathed in a rippling power field. Used most effectively when equipped in matched pairs, lightning claws are able to slice through armour, flesh and bone with terrifying effectiveness.

See the Warhammer 40,000 rulebook for details of using lightning claws.

Master-Crafted Weapons

Master-crafted weapons are each the product of years of careful labour by the most accomplished artisans in the Chapter. A weapon that has been manufactured with such dedication will be noticeably superior to any other weapon of its type.

A master-crafted weapon allows the bearer to re-roll one failed roll to hit per player turn when using the weapon.

Meltabomb

Meltabombs are subatomic charge-powered demolition munitions, capable of melting through even the most heavily armoured targets. Meltabombs are much bulkier than krak grenades, with a more sophisticated detonation mechanism, and so are only carried by specialist troops. Space Marine Assault squads carry melta bombs to destroy enemy tanks and bunkers.

See the Warhammer 40,000 rulebook for details of using meltabombs.

Meltagun

Meltaguns are lethal anti-armour weapons, used by Space Marines when undertaking assaults against heavily fortified defence lines and bastions. Most effective at very short range, the meltagun is capable of reducing rock, metal and living material to molten slag or ash.

Range	Strength	AP	Type
12"	8	1	Assault 1, Melta

Missile Launcher

The standard heavy weapon for Space Marine Tactical squads, missile launchers can fire either krak or frag missiles. Frag missiles are designed to wreak havoc amongst lightly armoured infantry, while krak missiles can challenge the most heavily armoured targets.

Each time a missile launcher fires, the controlling player must choose which type of missile is being used.

Frag

Range	Strength	AP	Type
48"	4	6	Heavy 1, Blast

Krak

Range	Strength	AP	Type
48"	8	3	Heavy 1

Multi-melta

A larger and longer-ranged version of the meltagun, a multi-melta is perfect for destroying bunkers and tanks.

Range	Strength	AP	Type
24"	8	1	Heavy 1, Melta

Plasma Cannon

Plasma cannons fire a plasma 'bolt' that explodes on impact, generating the destructive heat of a small sun. Plasma cannons are prone to overheating, and can prove as deadly to the wielder as the target.

Range	Strength	AP	Type
36"	7	2	Heavy 1, Blast, Gets Hot!

Plasma Gun

Smaller than the plasma cannon, a plasma gun fires several compact 'pulses' of searing plasma energy that are extremely effective against all manner of heavy infantry and light vehicles.

Range	Strength	AP	Type
24"	7	2	Rapid Fire, Gets Hot!

Plasma Pistol

Plasma pistols are the smallest variant in the plasma weapon family. Each shot from a plasma pistol contains all the destructive fury of a larger plasma gun, although with a reduced range and rate of fire.

A plasma pistol can be used as a close combat weapon, though it confers no Strength bonus or particular armour penetration advantages.

Range	Strength	AP	Type
12"	7	2	Pistol, Gets Hot!

Power Fist

A power fist is an armoured gauntlet surrounded by a disruptive energy field. It is used to deliver crushing blows, capable of smashing the thickest armour asunder.

See the Warhammer 40,000 rulebook for details of using power fists.

Power Weapon

A power weapon (typically a sword or axe, but sometimes a glaive, halberd or mace) is sheathed in the lethal haze of a disruptive energy field, capable of tearing through armour, flesh and bone with ease. See the Warhammer 40,000 rulebook for details of using power weapons.

Servo-arm

Techmarines and Servitors are equipped with powerful servo-arms that can be used for battlefield repairs or even put to use as a weapon. Each Servo-arm grants the model a single extra close combat attack, made separately at Initiative 1 and Strength 8, ignoring Armour Saves.

Servo-harness

A servo-harness gives the Techmarine an extra servo-arm (giving him two servo-arm attacks), a plasma cutter (fired in the Shooting phase as a twin-linked plasma pistol, but cannot be used in close combat) and a flamer. In the shooting phase the Techmarine can fire both harness-mounted weapons, or one harness mount and another gun.

Signum

The signum is a special form of communication device that can access a myriad of useful targeting data, allowing a more accurate concentration of fire. A model can use a signum in lieu of making a shooting attack of his own. If he does so, one model in his squad is Ballistic Skill 5 for the remainder of the Shooting phase. Declare that the signum is being used before any rolls to hit are made.

Shotgun

Shotguns are sturdy and versatile weapons often carried by Space Marine Scouts. They are invariably loaded with manstopper shells to provide extra punch.

Range	Strength	AP	Type
12"	4	-	Assault 2

Sniper Rifle

Sniper rifles boast powerful telescopic sights that enable the firer to target weak points and distant foes with unerring accuracy.

Range	Strength	AP	Type
36"	X	6	Heavy 1, Sniper

Storm Bolter

A storm bolter resembles two boltguns attached side by side. The storm bolter is capable of withering fire without hindering manoeuvrability, enabling the bearer to charge headlong into combat, firing on his enemy all the while.

Range	Strength	AP	Type
24"	4	5	Assault 2

Index of Further Weapons

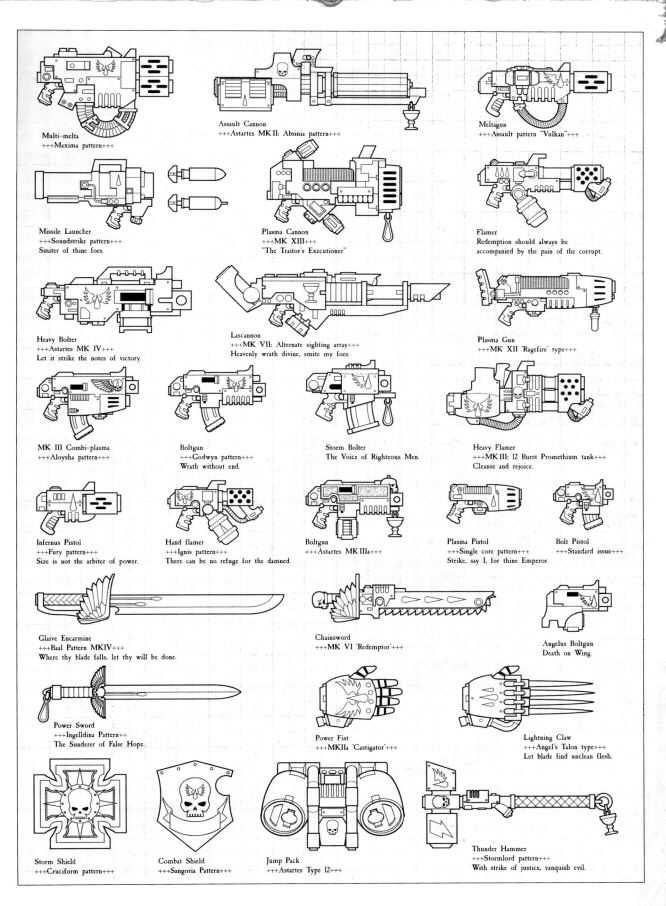

Multi-melta
+++Maxima pattern+++

Assault Cannon
+++Astartes MK II: Absinia pattern+++

Meltagun
+++Assault pattern "Vulkan"+++

Missile Launcher
+++Soundstrike pattern+++
Smiter of thine foes.

Plasma Cannon
+++MK XIII+++
"The Traitor's Executioner"

Flamer
Redemption should always be
accompanied by the pain of the corrupt.

Heavy Bolter
+++Astartes MK IV+++
Let it strike the notes of victory.

Lascannon
+++MK VII: Alternate sighting array+++
Heavenly wrath divine, smite my foes.

Plasma Gun
+++MK XII 'Ragefire' type+++

MK III Combi-plasma
+++Aloysha pattern+++

Boltgun
+++Godwyn pattern+++
Wrath without end.

Storm Bolter
The Voice of Righteous Men.

Heavy Flamer
+++MK III: 12 Burst Promethium tank+++
Cleanse and rejoice.

Infernus Pistol
+++Fury pattern+++
Size is not the arbiter of power.

Hand flamer
+++Ignis pattern+++
There can be no refuge for the damned.

Boltgun
+++Astartes MK IIIa+++

Plasma Pistol
+++Single core pattern+++
Strike, say I, for thine Emperor.

Bolt Pistol
+++Standard issue+++

Glaive Encarmine
+++Baal Pattern MKIV+++
Where thy blade falls, let thy will be done.

Chainsword
+++MK VI 'Redemptor'+++

Angelus Boltgun
Death on Wing.

Power Sword
+++Ingelldina Pattern++
The Sunderer of False Hope.

Power Fist
+++MKIIa 'Castigator'+++

Lightning Claw
+++Angel's Talon type+++
Let blade find unclean flesh.

Storm Shield
+++Cruciform pattern+++

Combat Shield
+++Sangoria Pattern+++

Jump Pack
+++Astartes Type 12+++

Thunder Hammer
+++Stormlord pattern+++
With strike of justice, vanquish evil.

VEHICLE EQUIPMENT

Autocannon

Autocannons are designed to destroy light vehicles and fire large calibre, high velocity shells. They are employed in the turret mounts of Predator Destructors, and are also carried, as a linked pair, on Dreadnoughts.

Range	Strength	AP	Type
48"	7	4	Heavy 2

Blood Fist

The blood fist is the standard close combat armament of many Blood Angels Dreadnoughts. A blood fist is a Dreadnought Close Combat weapon, as described in the Warhammer 40,000 rulebook. If a Dreadnought is equipped with a blood fist and a force weapon, it must choose which one it is going to use in each round of close combat, but will still gain one additional attack.

Blood Talon

With the unstoppable mass of a Dreadnought behind it, a single swipe from a blood talon can sweep aside a half dozen enemies – more, if the Dreadnought is wielding two such weapons. Blood talons follow the same rules as lightning claws. In addition, if the Dreadnought has two blood talons, the following rule applies: for every unsaved wound caused with a blood talon in close combat, the Dreadnought immediately makes an additional attack. These extra attacks can generate further additional attacks in the same way, until no further unsaved wounds are caused, or all the enemy are slain.

Demolisher Cannon

The demolisher cannon is the weapon of choice amongst the Imperium's armies when faced with dug-in enemy infantry in a dense environment such as a cityfight or a siege. The terrific blast unleashed by the detonation of the huge demolisher shells is often sufficient to bring down buildings in which the enemy has taken cover, crushing them beneath tons of fallen masonry. The demolisher cannon has the following profile:

Range	Strength	AP	Type
24"	10	2	Ordnance 1

Dozer Blade

Dozer blades are heavy ploughs, blades or rams, used to clear obstacles from the vehicle's path, Vehicles equipped with dozer blades can re-roll failed Difficult Terrain tests.

Extra Armour

Some Space Marine crews add additional armour plating to their vehicles to provide extra protection. Vehicles equipped with extra armour count "Crew Stunned" results on the Vehicle Damage tables as a "Crew Shaken" result instead.

Frag Assault Launchers

The hulls of Land Raider Crusaders and Land Raider Redeemers are studded with explosive charges designed to hurl shrapnel at the enemy as the troops inside charge out. Any unit charging into close combat on the same turn as it disembarks from a Land Raider Crusader or Redeemer counts as having frag grenades.

Frag Cannon

The frag cannon is utilised almost exclusively by the Blood Angels venerated Furioso Dreadnoughts. Its payload is a pair of double-shotted cylindrical adamantine shells, each the length of a Battle-Brother's arm. When fired, the hollow shell disintegrates into a hail of razor-sharp shards which gout forth from the cannon's mouth to shred armoured and unarmoured foes alike.

Range	Strength	AP	Type
Template	6	-	Assault 2, Rending

Hunter-killer Missile

Hunter-killer missiles are commonly fitted to the Imperium's vehicles. These single-use weapon systems allow vehicles such as Rhinos to engage enemy armoured vehicles that would otherwise far outmatch them.

A hunter-killer missile is a krak missile with unlimited range that can only be used once per battle. They are fired at Ballistic Skill 4 and are treated as an additional weapon.

Hurricane Bolters

Each hurricane bolter consists of three twin-linked bolters, fired as a single weapon.

Magna-Grapple

This Dreadnought weapon comprises a grapple and several yards of tempered adamantium chain. When fired at a vehicle, the grapple's magnetic and gravitic field generators form an unyielding bond with the target's hull, allowing the Dreadnought to 'drag' its prey closer.

Range	Strength	AP	Type
12"	8	2	Heavy 1, Grapple*

*Grapple: If the Magna-Grapple shot hits a vehicle and the target is not destroyed, roll a D6 and add 8 to the score. If the result is lower than the target's highest armour value, nothing happens – the Dreadnought doesn't have the leverage to reel the vehicle in.

If the result is equal to or higher than the target's highest armour value, the Dreadnought hauls the grapple in, dragging the vehicle with it. Move the vehicle 2D6" directly towards the Dreadnought.

The target does not change facing and will stop if it comes to within 1" of difficult terrain, impassable terrain, another vehicle (friendly or enemy) or a unit locked in close combat. Treat any non-vehicle unit the target moves over as having been tank-shocked. Once the drag has been completed, the Dreadnought releases the grapple – if the target survives the ensuing assault phase, it'll be able to move normally in its next turn.

Storm Bolter

Pintle-mounted storm bolters are weapons fitted to Space Marine vehicles to provide additional fire support. Pintle-mounted storm bolters are treated as an additional defensive weapon, with the profile of a normal storm bolter. See the storm bolter entry for details.

Searchlight

Searchlights are often fitted to Space Marine vehicles, so that the foe may not use darkness as an ally. Searchlights are used where the night fighting rule is in effect. If a vehicle has a searchlight it must still use the night fighting rules to pick a target but, having acquired a target, will illuminate it with the searchlight. For the rest of the Shooting phase, any other unit that fires at the illuminated unit does not use the night fighting special rule. However, a vehicle that uses a searchlight, can be targeted during the following enemy turn, as if the night fighting rules were not in effect, as the enemy can see the searchlight.

Siege Shield

Many Vindicators are equipped with one of these enormous bulldozer blades. A Vindicator with a siege shield automatically passes dangerous terrain tests.

Index of Further Vehicle Equipment

Smoke Launchers

Smoke launchers are used to temporarily obscure the vehicle behind concealing clouds of smoke. See the Warhammer 40,000 rulebook for details.

Whirlwind Multiple Missile Launcher

Each Whirlwind in your army is equipped with the standard vengeance missiles and the incendiary Castellan missiles. Declare which type of missile you wish to use before the Whirlwind fires.

Vengeance Missiles

Range	Strength	AP	Type
12-48"	5	4	Ordnance 1, Barrage

Incendiary Castellan Missiles

Range	Strength	AP	Type
12-48"	4	5	Ordnance 1, Barrage, Ignores cover*

*Ignores Cover: Cover saves cannot be taken against wounds caused by incendiary missiles.

ARMOUR

Artificer Armour

The superdense construction materials ensure that most suits of artificer armour offer a degree of protection rivalling that of Tactical Dreadnought armour. Models equipped with artificer armour receive an armour save of 2+.

Power Armour

Made from thick ceramite plates and electrically motivated fibre bundles that enhance the movements of the wearer, power armour is the standard protection for Space Marines. Models equipped with power armour receive an armour save of 3+.

Scout Armour

Scout armour is formed of thick plates of carapace armour, easily capable of stopping a bullet. Less cumbersome than power armour, scout armour is ideal for infiltration work and allows a greater freedom of motion. Models with Scout armour receive a 4+ armour save.

Terminator Armour

Terminator armour is the best protection a Space Marine can be equipped with. It is even said that Terminator armour can withstand the titanic energies at a plasma generator's core, and that this was in fact the armour's original purpose.

Due to the powerful exoskeleton and power sources built into their armour, models in Terminator armour have the relentless universal special rule. However, this armour is somewhat cumbersome, so Terminators cannot perform a Sweeping Advance.

A model wearing Terminator armour has a 2+ armour save and a 5+ invulnerable save. Any model wearing Terminator armour can be teleported onto the battlefield. They may always start the game in reserve and arrive using the Deep Strike rules, even if it is not part of the mission being played. Terminators count as two models for the purposes of transport capacity, and cannot embark Rhinos or Razorbacks.

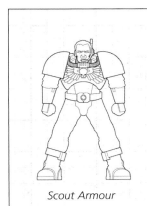

Scout Armour

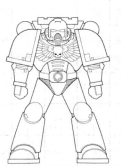

Power Armour

Artificer Armour

Terminator Armour

EQUIPMENT

Camo Cloak

Space Marine Scouts often wear camo cloaks – loose garments woven from light-absorbing material, that imitate surrounding terrain. So garbed, Scouts are almost impossible to see at long distance, and make for difficult targets when in cover of any kind.

A model wearing a camo cloak has the Stealth universal special rule.

Cluster Mines

When operating behind enemy lines, Scout Bikers carry cluster mines – explosive devices crammed with tiny anti-personnel bomblets and triggered by tripwires or pressure sensors. They are deployed in defensible positions to deny their use to all but the bravest or most foolhardy of foes.

Each Scout Bike squad equipped with cluster mines can booby-trap one piece of area terrain before the game begins. Note that a Scout Bike squad that splits into combat squads is still counted as a single squad for the purposes of cluster mines. At the start of the game, after terrain is placed, declare that your Scout Bikers have placed booby-traps and secretly write down the piece(s) of area terrain that have been booby-trapped in this fashion. Each terrain piece can only be booby-trapped once.

Cluster mines are automatically triggered the first time a unit (friendly or enemy) moves into the booby-trapped terrain. When triggered, the cluster mines inflict 2D6 hits on the unfortunate unit once it has finished its move. These are treated as shooting hits and use the following profile:

Range	Strength	AP	Type
n/a	4	-	No cover saves

If a vehicle triggers the cluster mines, the hits are always resolved against rear armour, to represent the munitions striking at its weaker under-armour. Once the effect of the cluster mines has been resolved, they are assumed to have been expended and have no further effect.

Combat Shield

A combat shield is a lighter version of a storm shield that is fitted to the arm of the wearer. This leaves the user's hand free to wield a pistol or other weapon, substituting a measure of defence for increased versatility. The combat shield confers a 6+ invulnerable save to its bearer.

Jump Pack

A jump pack enables the wearer to make great bounding leaps across the battlefield or even to fly short distances.

Models equipped with jump packs are jump infantry, as described in the Warhammer 40,000 rulebook. Space Marines wearing jump packs can be dropped from low-flying Thunderhawk Gunships, using their jump packs to swoop down on to the battlefield. To represent this they can be kept in reserve and arrive using the deep strike rules. In addition, a Blood Angels model with a jump pack has the Descent of Angels special rule (see page 23).

Space Marine Bike

Space Marine bikes are fitted with powerful engines and bulletproof tyres. Each bike is a versatile fighting platform capable of firing its armament on the move and launching devastating charges into combat. Models equipped with Space Marine Bikes follow all of the rules for bikes as described in the Warhammer 40,000 rulebook. Space Marine Bikes are fitted with a twin-linked bolter.

Storm Shield

A storm shield is a solid shield that has an energy field generator built into it. The energy field is capable of deflecting almost any attack, even blows from lascannons and power weapons.

A model with storm shield has a 3+ invulnerable save. A model equipped with a storm shield can never claim the +1 Attack bonus for being armed with two close combat weapons in an assault.

Teleport Homer

Teleport homers emit a powerful signal enabling Space Marine Strike Cruisers to lock on to them with their teleportation equipment. By utilising this signal, the risk of missing the intended mark is greatly reduced, as are the dangers of more serious accidents. If Terminators wish to teleport onto the battlefield via deep strike and choose to do so within 6" of a model carrying the homer, then they won't scatter. Note that the teleport homer only works for units that are teleporting, not for units entering play using jump packs, drop pods or other means of transport. Also note that the homer must already be on the table at the start of the turn for it to be used.

Index of Further Equipment

PSYCHIC POWERS

Other than Mephiston, every Blood Angels Librarian has two psychic powers (chosen when the army is picked). A Librarian can only use one power each player turn unless he has been upgraded to an Epistolary, in which case he can use up to two psychic powers each turn. All Blood Angels Librarian psychic powers are used following the rules given in the Warhammer 40,000 rulebook.

Blood Boil
The Librarian drives his enemy's blood into a seething frenzy, causing it to burst from every pore with explosive finality.

This power is a psychic shooting attack that hits automatically an enemy unit within 12". One model in that unit suffers a wound with no armour saves allowed. The victim of Blood Boil is chosen by your opponent, unless the total of the dice rolled for the psychic test is 5 or less, in which case the Librarian's controlling player chooses.

Fear of the Darkness
Summoning the indescribable malice of the Warp, the Librarian unleashes a mighty wave of sheer terror, assailing his foe's soul with nameless torment.

This power is a psychic shooting attack that hits automatically an enemy unit within 24". That unit must immediately take a Morale test with a -2 penalty to their Leadership. All normal modifiers and/or exceptions apply (e.g. units that never fall back are immune to this power).

Might of Heroes
The deadly powers of the Immaterium flow into the Librarian, heightening his speed and strength to unimaginable levels to smite the foes of the Emperor.

This power is used at the start of either player's Assault phase, and if successful, the Librarian (or any one other model in the same unit as the Librarian) gains +D3 attacks in that Assault phase.

Shackle Soul
The Librarian reaches into the foe's mind, trammelling his soul and crushing his will to fight.

This power is a psychic shooting attack that hits automatically an enemy unit within 12". Until the end of its next turn, the target unit must pass a Leadership test each time it wishes to move, run, shoot or assault – if the test is failed, the action cannot be performed. A unit that fails a test to run cannot instead choose to shoot, and vice versa.

Shield of Sanguinius
The Librarian wills a shimmering golden barrier into existence, preserving his companions from harm.

This power is used at the start of the enemy Shooting phase. The Librarian and any unit within 6" receive a 5+ cover save until the end of the phase.

Smite
Lethal bolts of ruby lightning leap from the Librarian's fingertips, tearing his enemies apart.

This power is a psychic shooting attack that has the following profile:

Range	Strength	AP	Type
12"	4	2	Assault 4

The Blood Lance
The Librarian conjures a mighty lance, glistening with gore. On a single word of command, the lance flies from his hands, skewering everything in its path.

This power is a psychic shooting attack. Extend a straight line, 4D6" long, from the Librarian's base in any direction – this is the path taken by the Blood Lance. Any enemy unit in the lance's path suffers a single Strength 8, AP 1 hit with the 'lance' type. Friendly units, and enemy units locked in close combat, are unaffected – the lance darts over them before continuing on its course.

The Sanguine Sword
The Librarian's force weapon takes on a violent crimson hue as he infuses it with a sliver of his inner rage.

This power is used at the start of either player's Assault phase. The Librarian's close combat attacks are made at Strength 10.

Unleash Rage
Reaching into the minds of his fellows, the Librarian unleashes the savagery within the Blood Angels' psyche.

This power is used at the start of either player's Assault phase. The Librarian and his unit have the Preferred Enemy special rule until the end of the turn.

Wings of Sanguinius
Two blood-red wings of psychic energy spring from the Librarian's back, allowing him to fly over the battlefield.

This power is used in the Librarian's Movement phase and lasts for the rest of the turn. It allows the Librarian to move as if he had a jump pack. A Librarian riding a bike that uses the Wings of Sanguinius moves as if he was riding a jet bike.

WARRIORS OF BAAL

It's time to begin assembling your angelic host, but where should you start? Fortunately, ten thousand years of war have served to highlight a few hints and tips for a new Blood Angels commander. Blood Angels are an assault force through and through. They have more close combat specialists than almost any other army. While not every Blood Angels troop type is intended for melee, those units not directly geared for close quarters have unique abilities that allow them to keep pace with your assault troops.

THE CORE OF YOUR STRIKE FORCE

The starting point for any army lies with its Troops choices. These represent the backbone of your strike force – careful selection here will put your feet on the road to victory.

As far as your other Troops choices go, a Tactical squad is a great all-round unit, able to dish out and withstand a fair amount of damage at all ranges. Assault squads, as their name suggests, excel in close quarters at the expense of firepower. Though somewhat fragile by the standards of Space Marines, Scouts are still comparable to the elites of other armies, and bring a range of special skills to the fray.

Of all the Troops at your disposal, the Death Company are unique – no other army in all of Warhammer 40,000 has anything like them. In terms of raw killing power, the Death Company put all other Assault squads to shame, whether you're butchering an Ork horde or slaughtering a Chaos Space Marine warband. Of course, this extra muscle comes at a price. A Death Company squad costs almost twice as many points as an equivalent-sized Assault squad. Nonetheless, nothing throws a scare into your opponent quite so much as the sight of the Death Company, and this psychological advantage is almost priceless! If you do select the Death Company, you might also want to purchase a Chaplain (from your Elites choices) to give them a little extra punch. Also remember that the Death Company cannot seize objectives – they're there to kill, not to capture.

There are, of course, no right or wrong choices – if in doubt, go with the models you like most.

ARCHANGELS

You'll also need at least one HQ choice to lead your army, which in the Blood Angels means a Captain, Librarian, Reclusiarch or one of several mighty special characters. Captains are the most flexible option, able to choose from a wide variety of wargear. Reclusiarchs are good augmentation characters, enhancing the fighting skills of those around them. Librarians lean less towards tactics and more to raw psychic power, whilst the special characters – famous heroes of the Chapter all – bring their own special skills to the fray.

ROUNDING OUT THE HOST

With your mandatory Troops and HQ filled out, it's worth casting an appraising eye towards selecting the rest of your mighty strike force. As with all Space Marine armies, the Blood Angels have a vast array of support troops to choose from. This can seem quite daunting at first, so it's worth taking a look at the following suggested army builds to get you started.

All Out Assault: If you want to play squarely to the Blood Angels' strengths, then an all-out assault army is for you. There's little subtlety here – include as large a Death Company as you can afford, and pack in as many Assault squads and Death Company Dreadnoughts as possible. If you choose Assault squads, Sanguinary Priests are a good addition – they can keep your Battle Brothers alive as they charge through the torrent of enemy fire. You should also consider several Chaplains – the Liturgies of Blood special rule drastically increases any squad's close combat ability.

The Heavenly Host: By adding several Sanguinary Guard and Vanguard Veteran squads to a core of Assault squads, you can quickly build a swift-moving and devastating jump infantry force. With judicious deployment of infernus pistols and hand flamers, you can guarantee that your army will be able to take on all-comers. Traditionally, the downside to jump infantry armies is their tendency to arrival piecemeal from deep strike, but this isn't an issue for the Blood Angels, thanks to their Descent of Angels special rule.

The Spear of Sanguinius: As all the Rhino variant tanks in the Blood Angels army are fast vehicles, there's a manoeuvrable, yet rugged tank spearhead to be forged should you so choose. Baal Predators are perhaps the ultimate word in close-quarter infantry extermination, although you might want to consider a Vindicator for annihilating more heavily armoured targets or a Whirlwind to strike from a distance. As ever, you'll need a couple of Troops choices, so consider embarking a couple of Tactical squads into Rhinos or Razorbacks – they can act as outriders for your other tanks or seize vital objectives depending on the course of battle.

The Chapter Elite: Last, but not least, by selecting Commander Dante as an HQ choice, you can fill out your Troops choices with the golden glory of the Sanguinary Guard, leaving you free to expend your Elites slots on Terminators or perhaps a Furioso Dreadnought or two. All of these selections have a suitably high points cost, so your army will be especially elite and compact. As a result, you'll want to make full use of any cover as you cross the battlefield – once you hit home against the enemy lines you'll inflict unimaginable carnage!

CHAPTER AND HERALDRY

Though this Codex focuses on the Blood Angels, the army list can be used to create strike forces from their Successor Chapters as well. You'll find plenty of colour schemes and iconography examples on the following pages. Many gamers like to follow these examples, but don't be afraid to create a new Chapter of your own and forge a fresh legend with every battle. Further information on painting your army can be found in the How to Paint Citadel Miniatures, How to Paint Space Marines and How to Paint Citadel Tanks books.

Led by the Sanguinor, the Blood Angels host descends upon an Iron Warriors fortress.

The Sanguinor, Exemplar of the Host.

Captain Erasmus Tycho.

Commander Dante,
Chapter Master of the Blood Angels.

Blood Angels Captain.

Gabriel Seth, Chapter Master of the Flesh Tearers.

Brother Corbulo.

Mephiston, Lord of Death.

Blood Angels Librarian.

Sanguinary Guard.

Sanguinary Guard standard bearer.

Sanguinary Guard.

Sanguinary Guards.

Sanguinary Novitiate.

Honour Guard.

Honour Guard.

Honour Guard with Chapter Banner.

Blood Champion.

Like most Space Marine Chapters, the Blood Angels have many different Chapter Banners, each commemorating a mighty victory or particularly pivotal campaign. Each Chapter Banner carries a stylised image of Sanguinius, with the exact detail of his weaponry and accoutrements a reference to the event the banner celebrates.

Company banners are emblazoned not only with the symbols of the company, but they also display the personal heraldry of the commanding officer, as well as army badges, battle assignments and other honours. Many of the company banners have been present at some of the Imperium's bloodiest battles.

Honour Guard with company banner.

Many Blood Angels officers and sergeants carry banners displaying their own personal heraldry. These will often have been crafted by the warrior in question in the brief lulls between wars.

The heraldry of the famed Death Company Dreadnought Metraen displays the triple blood drop and grail motifs that adorned its pilot Moriar's back banner when he led the 4th Company to battle.

Tycho's back banner incorporates a red stripe and bloody wing, echoed on his company's banner.

The banners of Blood Angels Chaplains invariably contain winged skeletal heralds that serve as grim reminders of the Flaw that all Blood Angels are heir to.

Banner presented to Mephiston following his heroic exploits on the hive world of Hollonan.

Terminators with lightning claws.

Terminator with thunder hammer and storm shield.

Terminator Sergeant with thunder hammer and storm shield.

Terminator with heavy flamer and power fist.

Terminator Sergeant with storm bolter and power sword.

Terminator with storm bolter and power fist.

Terminators with storm bolters and chainfists.

Sergeant Lorenzo, from 'Space Hulk', released 2009.

Veteran Sergeant with boltgun and power fist.

Sternguard Veterans with boltguns.

Sternguard Veteran with combi-melta.

Tactical Space Marines with boltguns.

Tactical Space Marines with boltguns.

Space Marine Sergeant with power fist and bolt pistol.

Tactical Space Marine with multi-melta.

Tactical Space Marine with meltagun.

Scout with sniper rifle.   *Scout with heavy bolter.*   *Scout Sergeant.*   *Scouts with shotguns.*

Blood Angels Tactical Sergeant.

Blood Angels Assault Marine.

Blood Angels Devastator Marine.

Blood Angels Veteran.

Company badge displayed on right shoulder pad:

1st Company Badge
White/Silver.

2nd Company Badge
Yellow/Gold.

3rd Company Badge
White/Silver.

4th Company Badge
Green/Adamantite.

5th Company Badge
Black/Ebonite.

6th Company Badge
Yellow/Gold.

7th Company Badge
White/Silver.

8th Company Badge
Green/Adamantite.

9th Company Badge
Black/Ebonite.

10th Company Badge
Black/Ebonite.

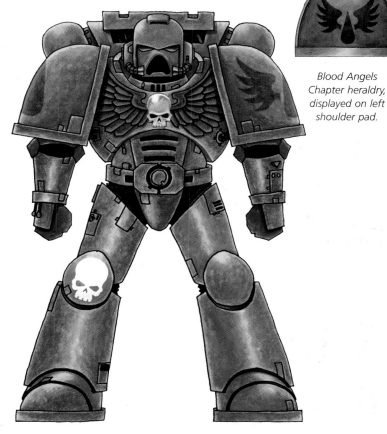

Blood Angels
Chapter heraldry,
displayed on left
shoulder pad.

Blood Angels Tactical Space Marine
from the 2nd Squad, 5th Company.

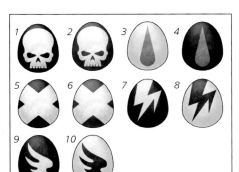
Blood Angels squad markings, commonly
displayed on the right knee pad. Squad
numbers given above.

Sanguinary Guard.

Death Company.

Astorath the Grim.

Lemartes, Guardian of the Lost.

Death Company with boltguns.

Death Company Assault Marine with thunder hammer.

Death Company Assault Marine with infernus pistol.

Captain Tycho after his induction into the Death Company.

Death Company Assault Marine with power sword and bolt pistol.

Death Company Assault Marine with chainsword and bolt pistol.

Death Company Assault Marine with power fist and bolt pistol.

Assault Marine with chainsword and hand flamer.

Assault Sergeant with power weapon and infernus pistol.

Assault Marines with bolt pistols and chainswords.

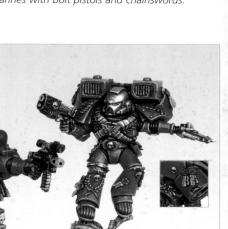

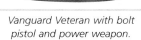
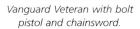

Vanguard Veteran with plasma pistol and chainsword.

Vanguard Veteran with bolt pistol and power weapon.

Vanguard Veteran with bolt pistol and chainsword.

Vanguard Veteran with plasma pistol and chainsword.

Chaplain Lemartes leads the Death Company against the Tyranid swarm.

Dreadnought with multi-melta and blood fist with built-in storm bolter.

Furioso Dreadnought with two blood fists.

Death Company Dreadnought with two blood talons.

Rhino armoured transport.

Razorback with twin-linked heavy bolter and storm bolter.

Death Company Rhino.

Space Marine Biker.

Space Marine Biker with meltagun.

Space Marine Biker Sergeant
with power sword.

Space Marine Attack Bike.

Scout Biker.

A Blood Angels armoured strike force.

Baal Predator with twin-linked assault cannons and heavy bolter sponsons.

Baal Predator with flamestorm cannon and heavy flamer sponsons.

Land Speeder with multi-melta.

Devastators with plasma cannons. Devastator with boltgun. Devastator with missile launcher. Devastator with boltgun.

Devastator Sergeant. Devastator with multi-melta. Techmarine with jump pack.

Land Raider Redeemer.

Predator with autocannon turret and heavy bolter sponsons.

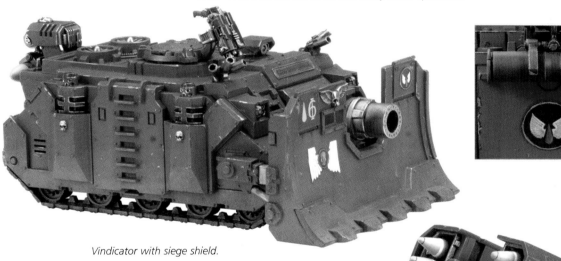

Vindicator with siege shield.

Whirlwind.

The Blood Angels have spawned many Successor Chapters who follow their precursor's heraldic schemes, just as they do their traditions. Only the Blood Drinkers use the heraldic patterns exactly as laid down in the Codex Astartes.

Angels Sanguine.

Flesh Tearers.

Lamenters.

Angels Encarmine.

Knights of Blood.

Blood Drinkers.

Angels Vermillion.

The Successor Chapters invariably maintain a Sanguinary Guard and Death Company of their own, following the same colour schemes as those laid down by the Blood Angels. The only exception are the Angels Encarmine who adorn both these specialist units in alabaster white armour – shown right.

Angels Sanguine.

Flesh Tearers.

Lamenters.

Angels Encarmine.

Knights of Blood.

Blood Drinkers.

Angels Vermillion.

BLOOD ANGELS ARMY LIST

The following army list enables you to field a Blood Angels army and fight battles using the scenarios included in the Warhammer 40,000 rulebook.

USING THE ARMY LIST

The Blood Angels army list is split into five sections: HQ, Elites, Troops, Fast Attack and Heavy Support. All of the squads, vehicles and characters in the army are placed into one of these sections depending upon their role on the battlefield. Each model is also given a points value, which varies depending on how effective that model is in battle.

Before you choose an army, you will need to agree with your opponent upon the type of game you are going to play and the maximum total number of points each of you will spend. Then you can proceed to pick your army.

USING A FORCE ORGANISATION CHART

The army list is used in conjunction with the force organisation chart from a scenario. Each chart is split into five categories that correspond to the sections in the army list, and each category has one or more boxes. Each grey-toned box indicates that you may make one choice from that section of the army list, while a dark-toned box indicates a compulsory selection.

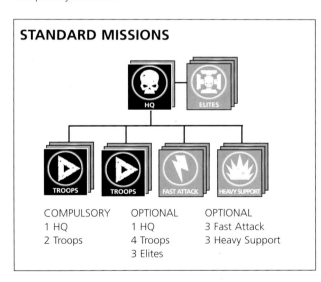

STANDARD MISSIONS

COMPULSORY	OPTIONAL	OPTIONAL
1 HQ	1 HQ	3 Fast Attack
2 Troops	4 Troops	3 Heavy Support
	3 Elites	

ARMY LIST ENTRIES

Each entry in the army list represents a different unit. More information about the background and rules for the Blood Angels and their options can be found in the Angelic Host section, while examples of the Citadel miniatures you will need to represent them can be found in the Warriors of Baal section.

Each unit entry in the Blood Angels army list is split into several sections:

Unit Name: At the start of each army list entry you will find the name of the unit alongside the points cost of the unit without any upgrades.

Unit Profile: This section will show the profile of any models the unit can include.

Unit Composition: Where applicable, this section will show the number and type of models that make up the basic unit, before any upgrades are taken. If the Unit Composition includes the word 'Unique', then you may only include one of this unit in your army.

Unit Type: This refers to the Warhammer 40,000 Unit Type Rules chapter. For example, a unit may be classed as infantry, vehicle or cavalry, which will subject it to a number of rules regarding movement, shooting, assault, etc.

Wargear: This section details the weapons and equipment the models in the unit are armed with. The cost for all these models and their equipment is included in the points cost listed next to the unit name.

Special Rules: Any special rules that apply to the models in the unit are listed here. These special rules are explained in further detail in either the Angelic Host section or the Universal Special Rules section of the Warhammer 40,000 rulebook.

Dedicated Transport: Where applicable, this section refers to any transport vehicles the unit may take. These have their own army list entry on page 90-91. The Transport Vehicles section of the Warhammer 40,000 rulebook explains how these dedicated transport vehicles work.

Options: This section lists all of the upgrades you may add to the unit if you wish to do so alongside the associated points cost for each. Where an option states that you may exchange one weapon 'and/or' another, you may replace either, neither or both provided you pay the points cost.

Blood Angels and other chapters

This army list is based first and foremost around the Blood Angels, but can also be used to collect an army based around one of their Successor chapters. Use the Blood Angels army list presented on the following pages and paint your miniatures using one of the colour schemes shown in this book (or create the colours and heraldry yourself).

This should not prevent you using one or more of the Blood Angels special characters (or indeed from using Gabriel Seth, a Flesh Tearers character, alongside a Blood Angels army). They can still be used in the same army, representing the common occurrence of different chapters fighting alongside one another. Alternatively, you can use the model and rules for a named character to represent a mighty hero of a different chapter – for example, using the rules and model for Captain Tycho as a Blood Drinkers Captain, or of a Space Marine chapter of your own design – you just need to come up with a new name.

This is a perfect way to personalise your army – just make sure your opponent is aware of what everything counts as before the beginning of the game to prevent confusion during the battle.

HQ

COMMANDER DANTE .... 225 Points   **Page 53**

	WS	BS	S	T	W	I	A	Ld	Sv
Commander Dante	6	5	4	4	4	6	4	10	2+

Unit Composition:
- 1 (Unique)

Unit Type:
- Jump infantry

Master of the Host
In an army that includes Commander Dante, Sanguinary Guard are Troops choices.

Wargear:
- Artificer armour
- Infernus pistol
- The Axe Mortalis
- Jump pack
- Frag and krak grenades
- Iron Halo
- Death Mask of Sanguinius

Special Rules:
- And They Shall Know No Fear
- Descent of Angels
- Independent Character
- Surgical Strike
- Tactical Precision

CHAPTER MASTER GABRIEL SETH .... 160 Points   **Page 55**

	WS	BS	S	T	W	I	A	Ld	Sv
Gabriel Seth	6	5	4	4	4	5	4	10	3+

Unit Composition:
- 1 (Unique)

Unit Type:
- Infantry

Wargear:
- Power armour
- Bolt pistol
- Blood Reaver
- Frag and krak grenades
- Iron Halo

Special Rules:
- Fearless
- Ferocious Instincts
- Independent Character
- Whirlwind of Gore

ASTORATH THE GRIM .... 220 Points   **Page 45**

	WS	BS	S	T	W	I	A	Ld	Sv
Astorath	6	5	4	4	3	5	3	10	2+

Unit Composition:
- 1 (Unique)

Unit Type:
- Jump infantry

Redeemer of the Lost
In an army that includes Astorath the Grim, the 0-1 Death Company limit is removed.

Wargear:
- Artificer armour
- Bolt pistol
- The Executioner's Axe
- Frag and krak grenades
- Jump pack
- Rosarius

Special Rules:
- Descent of Angels
- Independent Character
- Liturgies of Blood
- Honour of the Chapter
- Shadow of the Primarch

THE SANGUINOR, EXEMPLAR OF THE HOST .... 275 Points   **Page 51**

	WS	BS	S	T	W	I	A	Ld	Sv
Sanguinor	8	5	5	4	3	6	5	10	2+

Unit Composition:
- 1 (Unique)

Unit Type:
- Jump infantry

Wargear:
- Artificer armour
- Glaive Encarmine
- Frag and krak grenades
- Jump pack

Special Rules:
- Descent of Angels
- Aura of Fervour
- Avenging Angel
- Eternal Warrior
- Fearless
- Furious Charge
- The Sanguinor's Blessing
- Unyielding Will

MEPHISTON, LORD OF DEATH .... 250 Points   **Page 47**

	WS	BS	S	T	W	I	A	Ld	Sv
Mephiston	7	5	6	6	5	7	4	10	2+

Unit Composition:
- 1 (Unique)

Unit Type:
- Infantry

Psychic Powers:
- The Sanguine Sword
- Unleash Rage
- Wings of Sanguinius

Wargear:
- Artificer armour
- Plasma pistol
- Force sword
- Frag and krak grenades
- Psychic hood

Special Rules:
- And They Shall Know No Fear
- Fleet
- Psyker
- Transfixing Gaze

HQ

CAPTAIN TYCHO .... 175 Points

	WS	BS	S	T	W	I	A	Ld	Sv
Captain Tycho	6	5	4	4	3	5	3	10	2+
Death Company Tycho	7	4	4	4	3	5	4	8	2+

Unit Composition:
• 1 (Unique)

Unit Type:
• Infantry

You must choose which version of Tycho you wish to use when you select your army.

Wargear:
• Artificer armour
• Blood Song
• Bolt pistol
• The Dead Man's Hand
• Frag and krak grenades
• Iron Halo

Special Rules (Captain):
• And They Shall Know No Fear
• Independent Character
• Preferred Enemy: Orks
• Rites of Battle

Special Rules (Death Company):
• Black Rage
• Fearless
• Feel No Pain
• Fleet
• Furious Charge
• Preferred Enemy: Orks
• Relentless

LIBRARIAN .... 100 Points

Page 46

	WS	BS	S	T	W	I	A	Ld	Sv
Librarian	5	4	4	4	2	4	2	10	3+

Unit Composition:
• 1 Librarian

Unit Type:
• Infantry

Wargear:
• Power armour
• Boltgun or bolt pistol
• Frag and krak grenades
• Force weapon
• Psychic hood

Special Rules:
• And They Shall Know No Fear
• Independent Character
• Psyker

Psychic Powers:
A Librarian has any two of the following powers: *Blood Boil, Fear of the Darkness, Might of Heroes, Shackle Soul, Shield of Sanguinius, Smite, The Blood Lance, The Sanguine Sword, Unleash Rage, Wings of Sanguinius.*

Options:
• Upgrade to an Epistolary .... +50 pts
• Replace boltgun and/or bolt pistol with:
  - a storm bolter .... +3 pts
  - a hand flamer or combi-flamer, -melta or -plasma +10 pts
  - a plasma pistol or infernus pistol .... +15 pts
• Replace power armour, boltgun, frag and krak grenades for Terminator armour and:
  - no additional weapon .... +25 pts
  - a storm bolter .... +30 pts
  - a combi-flamer, -melta or -plasma .... +35 pts
  - a storm shield .... +45 pts
• If Terminator armour is not chosen, can have one of the following:
  - Jump pack .... +25 pts
  - Space Marine bike .... +35 pts

RECLUSIARCH .... 130 Points

Page 42

	WS	BS	S	T	W	I	A	Ld	Sv
Reclusiarch	5	5	4	4	3	5	3	10	3+

Unit Composition:
• 1 Reclusiarch

Unit Type:
• Infantry

Wargear:
• Power armour
• Boltgun or bolt pistol
• Frag and krak grenades
• Rosarius
• Crozius Arcanum

Special Rules:
• Independent Character
• Liturgies of Blood
• Honour of the Chapter

Options:
• Replace boltgun and/or bolt pistol with:
  - a storm bolter .... +3 pts
  - a hand flamer or combi-flamer, -melta or -plasma +10 pts
  - a power fist, plasma pistol or infernus pistol .... +15 pts
• Take melta bombs .... +5 pts
• Replace power armour, boltgun, frag and krak grenades for Terminator armour and:
  - a storm bolter .... +30 pts
  - a combi-flamer, -melta or -plasma .... +35 pts
• If Terminator armour is not chosen, can have one of the following:
  - Jump pack .... +25 pts
  - Space Marine bike .... +35 pts

HQ

CAPTAIN ....100 Points   Page 40

	WS	BS	S	T	W	I	A	Ld	Sv
Captain	6	5	4	4	3	5	3	10	3+

Unit Composition:
• 1 Captain

Unit Type:
• Infantry

Wargear:
• Power armour
• Boltgun or bolt pistol
• Chainsword
• Frag and krak grenades
• Iron Halo

Special Rules:
• And They Shall Know No Fear
• Independent Character

Options:
• Replace boltgun, bolt pistol and/or chainsword with:
  - a storm bolter ....+3 pts
  - a hand flamer or combi-flamer, -melta or -plasma +10 pts
  - a power sword, lightning claw plasma pistol or infernus pistol ....+15 pts
  - a storm shield ....+20 pts
  - a power fist ....+25 pts
  - a thunder hammer ....+30 pts
• Take melta bombs ....+5 pts
• Replace power armour, boltgun, chainsword, frag and krak grenades with Terminator armour with storm bolter and power sword ....+40 pts
• Replace Terminator armour's storm bolter with:
  - combi-flamer, -melta or -plasma ....+5 pts
  - lightning claw ....+10 pts
  - thunder hammer ....+20 pts
• Replace Terminator armour's power sword with:
  - lightning claw ....+5 pts
  - power fist ....+10 pts
  - storm shield, thunder hammer or chainfist ....+15 pts
• If Terminator armour is not chosen, can have one of the following:
  - Jump pack ....+25 pts
  - Space Marine bike ....+35 pts

HONOUR GUARD ....115 Points   Page 52
You can take one unit of Honour Guard for every HQ unit you have included in your army, not counting Honour Guard units. Units of Honour Guard do not themselves take up an HQ choice.

	WS	BS	S	T	W	I	A	Ld	Sv
Honour Guard	4	4	4	4	1	4	2	9	3+
Blood Champion	5	4	4	4	1	4	2	9	3+
Sanguinary Novitiate	4	4	4	4	1	4	2	9	3+

Unit Composition:
• 4 Honour Guards
• 1 Sanguinary Novitiate

Unit Type:
• Infantry

Wargear:
• Power armour
• Boltgun or bolt pistol
• Chainsword
• Frag and krak grenades
• The Sanguinary Novitiate also has a Blood Chalice

Special Rules:
• And They Shall Know No Fear
• The Red Thirst

Dedicated Transport:
• If the squad does not have jump packs, it can select any dedicated transport (see page 90).

Options:
• One Honour Guard can be upgraded to a Blood Champion with power weapon and combat shield +20 pts
• One Honour Guard can carry either:
  - a Company Standard ....+15 pts
  - the Chapter Banner (only one per army, see Sanguinary Guard): ....+ 30 pts
• The entire squad can have jump packs: ....+50 pts
• Any Honour Guard can replace his boltgun, chainsword and/or bolt pistol with:
  - a storm bolter ....+3 pts per model
  - a flamer ....+5 pts per model
  - a meltagun, combi-flamer, -melta or -plasma or hand flamer ....+10 pts per model
  - a plasma gun, plasma pistol, infernus pistol, power sword or lightning claw ....+15 pts per model
  - a storm shield ....+20 pts per model
  - a power fist ....+25 pts per model
  - a thunder hammer ....+30 pts per model
• Any Honour Guard can have the following:
  - melta bombs ....+5 pts per model

ELITES

CHAPLAIN ....100 Points   Page 42

	WS	BS	S	T	W	I	A	Ld	Sv
Chaplain	5	4	4	4	2	4	2	10	3+

Unit Composition:
• 1 Chaplain

Unit Type:
• Infantry

Wargear:
• Power armour
• Boltgun or bolt pistol
• Frag and krak grenades
• Rosarius and Crozius Arcanum

Special Rules:
• Independent Character
• Honour of the Chapter
• Liturgies of Blood

Options:
• Replace boltgun and/or bolt pistol with:
  - a storm bolter ....+3 pts
  - a hand flamer, combi-flamer, -melta or -plasma ... +10 pts
  - a power fist, plasma pistol or infernus pistol ...... +15 pts
• Take melta bombs ....+5 pts
• Replace power armour, boltgun, frag and krak
  grenades for Terminator armour and:
  - a storm bolter ....+30 pts
  - a combi-flamer, -melta or -plasma ....+35 pts
• If Terminator armour is not chosen,
  can have one of the following:
  - Jump pack ....+25 pts
  - Space Marine bike ....+35 pts

SANGUINARY GUARD ....200 Points   Page 50

	WS	BS	S	T	W	I	A	Ld	Sv
Sanguinary Guard	4	4	4	4	1	4	2	10	2+

Unit Composition:
• 5 Sanguinary Guard

Unit Type:
• Jump Infantry

Wargear:
• Artificer armour
• Angelus boltgun
• Glaive Encarmine
• Frag and krak grenades
• Jump pack

Special Rules:
• Descent of Angels
• Fearless
• The Red Thirst

Options:
• The entire squad can be given Death Masks for .....+25 pts
• One Sanguinary Guard can carry the Chapter Banner
  (only one per army, see Honour Guard) ....+30 pts
• Any model can replace his Angelus boltgun with:
  - an infernus pistol or plasma pistol ......+10 pts per model
• Any model can replace his Glaive Encarmine with:
  - a power fist ....+10 pts per model

FURIOSO DREADNOUGHT ....125 Points   Page 29

				┌─ Armour ─┐				
	WS	BS	S	F	S	R	I	A
Furioso Dreadnought	6	4	6	13	12	10	4	2(3)

Unit Composition:
• 1 Dreadnought

Unit Type:
• Vehicle (Walker)

Wargear:
• Blood fist with
  built-in storm bolter
• Blood fist with
  built-in meltagun
• Smoke launchers

Special Rules:
• The Red Thirst

Dedicated Transport:
• Can select a Drop Pod
  (see page 90).

Psychic Powers:
A Furioso Librarian has any
two of the following
psychic powers:
*Blood Boil, Fear of the
Darkness, Might of Heroes,
Shackle Soul, Shield of
Sanguinius, Smite, The
Blood Lance, The Sanguine
Sword, Unleash Rage,
Wings of Sanguinius.*

Options:
• Replace one blood fist (and built-in weapon) with:
  a frag cannon ....free
• Replace both blood fists with a pair of blood talons
  (the built-in weapons are retained) ....free
• Replace storm bolter with heavy flamer ....+10 pts
• Take magna-grapple ....+15 pts
• Take extra armour ....+15 pts
• Take searchlight ....+1 pt
• Upgrade to a Furioso Librarian, exchanging all wargear
  for a blood fist (with built-in storm bolter), smoke
  launchers, psychic hood and force weapon ....+50 pts

ELITES

TERMINATOR SQUAD ....200 Points   Page 28

	WS	BS	S	T	W	I	A	Ld	Sv
Terminator	4	4	4	4	1	4	2	9	2+
Terminator Sergeant	4	4	4	4	1	4	2	9	2+

Unit Composition:
- 1 Terminator Sergeant
- 4 Terminators

Unit Type:
- Infantry

Wargear:
- Terminator armour
- Storm bolter
- Power fist
(the Sergeant has a
power sword instead).

Special Rules:
- And They Shall
Know No Fear
- Combat Squads
- The Red Thirst

Dedicated Transport:
- The squad can select a
Land Raider of any type
as a dedicated transport
(see page 91).

Options:
- Add up to five Terminators ....+40 pts per model
- For every five models in the squad, one Terminator can:
  - replace his storm bolter with a heavy flamer ....+5 pts
  - replace his storm bolter with an assault cannon ...+30 pts
  - take a cyclone missile launcher ....+30 pts
- Any Terminator can replace its power fist
with a chainfist: ....+5 pts per model

TERMINATOR ASSAULT SQUAD ....200 Points   Page 28

	WS	BS	S	T	W	I	A	Ld	Sv
Terminator	4	4	4	4	1	4	2	9	2+
Terminator Sergeant	4	4	4	4	1	4	2	9	2+

Unit Composition:
- 1 Terminator Sergeant
- 4 Terminators

Unit Type:
- Infantry

Wargear:
- Terminator armour
- Lightning claws

Special Rules:
- And They Shall
Know No Fear
- Combat Squads
- The Red Thirst

Dedicated Transport:
- The squad can select a
Land Raider of any type
as a dedicated transport
(see page 91).

Options:
- Add up to five Terminators ....+40 pts per model
- Any model can replace his lightning claws with a
thunder hammer and storm shield ....+5 pts per model

TECHMARINE ....50 Points   Page 39

	WS	BS	S	T	W	I	A	Ld	Sv
Techmarine	4	4	4	4	1	4	1	8	2+
Servitor	3	3	3	3	1	3	1	8	4+

Unit Composition:
- 1 Techmarine
- 0-5 Servitors

Unit Type:
- Infantry

Wargear (Techmarine):
- Artificer armour
- Servo-arm
- Boltgun or bolt pistol
- Frag and krak grenades

Wargear (Servitors):
- Close combat weapon
- Servo-arm

**Special Rules
(Techmarine):**
- And They Shall
Know No Fear
- Blessing of the Omnissiah
- Bolster Defences

Options:
- Exchange servo-arm for a jump pack ....free
- Upgrade servo-arm to a servo-harness ....+25 pts
- Replace boltgun with:
  - a storm bolter ....+3 pts
  - a combi-flamer, -melta or -plasma..................+10 pts
  - a plasma pistol ....+15 pts
- Take either:
  - a power weapon ....+15 pts
  - a thunder hammer ....+30 pts
- The Techmarine can be accompanied by
up to five Servitors ....+15 pts per model
- Up to two Servitors can replace their servo-arm with:
  - a heavy bolter ....+20 pts per model
  - a multi-melta or plasma cannon ....+30 pts per model

ELITES

STERNGUARD VETERAN SQUAD .... 125 Points

Page 27

	WS	BS	S	T	W	I	A	Ld	Sv
Veteran	4	4	4	4	1	4	2	9	3+
Space Marine Sergeant	4	4	4	4	1	4	2	9	3+

Unit Composition:
- 1 Space Marine Sergeant
- 4 Veterans

Unit Type:
- Infantry

Wargear:
- Power armour
- Boltgun
- Bolt pistol
- Special issue ammunition
- Frag and krak grenades

Special Rules:
- And They Shall Know No Fear
- Combat Squads
- The Red Thirst

Dedicated Transport:
- The squad can select any dedicated transport (see page 90).

Options:
- Add up to five Veterans .... +25 pts per model
- The Space Marine Sergeant can replace his bolt pistol and/or his boltgun with:
  - a chainsword .... free
  - a power weapon, plasma pistol or lightning claw .... +15 pts
  - a power fist .... +25 pts
- The Space Marine Sergeant can take:
  - melta bombs .... +5 pts
- Any model can replace his boltgun with:
  - a storm bolter, combi-melta, -flamer or -plasma .... +5 pts
- Two Veterans can replace their boltguns with:
  - a flamer, a meltagun, a heavy bolter, a multi-melta or a missile launcher .... +5 pts per model
  - a plasma gun, plasma cannon or heavy flamer .... +10 pts per model
  - a lascannon .... +15 pts per model

---

SANGUINARY PRIEST .... 50 Points

Page 48

You can take 1-3 Sanguinary Priests (one of which can be Brother Corbulo) as a single Elites choice.

	WS	BS	S	T	W	I	A	Ld	Sv
Sanguinary Priest	5	4	4	4	1	4	2	9	3+

Unit Composition:
- 1 Sanguinary Priest

Unit Type:
- Infantry

Wargear:
- Power armour
- Bolt pistol
- Chainsword
- Blood Chalice
- Frag and krak grenades

Special Rules:
- And They Shall Know No Fear
- Independent Character

Options:
- Replace bolt pistol with:
  - a storm bolter .... + 3 pts
  - a hand flamer, combi-flamer, -melta or -plasma ..+10 pts
  - a plasma pistol or infernus pistol .... +15 pts
- Replace chainsword with:
  - a power sword or lightning claw .... +15 pts
  - a power fist .... +25 pts
- Take melta bombs .... +5 pts
- Replace all wargear with Terminator armour with Chalice of Blood and power sword .... +35 pts
- If Terminator armour is not chosen, can have one of the following:
  - Jump pack .... +25 pts
  - Space Marine bike .... +35 pts

BROTHER CORBULO .... 105 Points

Page 49

You can include Brother Corbulo as one of your Sanguinary Priests.

	WS	BS	S	T	W	I	A	Ld	Sv
Corbulo	5	5	4	4	2	5	3	9	3+

Unit Composition:
- 1 (Unique)

Unit Type:
- Infantry

Wargear:
- Power armour
- Bolt pistol
- Heaven's Teeth
- Frag and krak grenades
- The Red Grail

Special Rules:
- And They Shall Know No Fear
- The Far-Seeing Eye
- Independent Character

TROOPS

TACTICAL SQUAD ....90 Points   Page 24

	WS	BS	S	T	W	I	A	Ld	Sv
Space Marine	4	4	4	4	1	4	1	8	3+
Space Marine Sergeant	4	4	4	4	1	4	2	9	3+

Unit Composition:
- 4 Space Marines
- 1 Space Marine Sergeant

Unit Type:
- Infantry

Wargear:
- Power armour
- Boltgun
- Bolt pistol
- Frag and krak grenades

Special Rules:
- And They Shall Know No Fear
- Combat Squads
- The Red Thirst

Dedicated Transport:
- The squad can select any dedicated transport (see page 90).

Options:
- Add up to five Space Marines ....+16 pts per model
- If the squad numbers ten models, one Space Marine can replace his boltgun with one of the following:
  - a flamer ....free
  - a meltagun ....+5 pts
  - a plasma gun ....+10 pts
- If the squad numbers ten models, one Space Marine can replace his boltgun with one of the following:
  - a heavy bolter, multi-melta or a missile launcher ....free
  - a plasma cannon ....+5 pts
  - a lascannon ....+10 pts
- The Space Marine Sergeant can replace his boltgun and/or bolt pistol with:
  - a chainsword...free
  - a storm bolter ....+3 pts
  - a combi-melta, -flamer or -plasma ....+10 pts
  - a plasma pistol or power weapon ....+15 pts
  - a power fist ....+25 pts
- The Space Marine Sergeant can take:
  - melta bombs...+5 pts
  - teleport homer ....+15 pts

DEATH COMPANY ....60 Points   Page 44
You can include only one unit of Death Company in your army.

	WS	BS	S	T	W	I	A	Ld	Sv
Death Company	5	4	4	4	1	4	2	8	3+

Unit Composition:
- 3 Death Company

Unit Type:
- Infantry

Wargear
- Power armour
- Boltgun or bolt pistol
- Chainsword
- Frag and krak grenades

Special Rules:
- Black Rage
- Fearless
- Feel No Pain
- Furious Charge
- Relentless

Dedicated Transport:
- If the squad does not have jump packs, it can select any dedicated transport (see page 90).

Options:
- Add up to twenty-seven Death Company:.............+20 pts per model
- Any Death Company can replace their bolt pistol and/or chainsword with:
  - a power weapon ....+15 pts per model
  - a power fist ....+25 pts per model
  - a thunder hammer ....+30 pts per model
- For every five models in the squad, one Death Company can replace his bolt pistol with one of the following:
  - a hand flamer ....+10 pts per model
  - an infernus pistol or plasma pistol .....+15 pts per model
- The entire squad can have jump packs: ..+15 pts per model

LEMARTES, GUARDIAN OF THE LOST ....150 Points   Page 43
The Death Company can include Lemartes.

	WS	BS	S	T	W	I	A	Ld	Sv
Lemartes	5	4	4	4	2	6	2	10	3+

Unit Composition:
- 1 (Unique)

Unit Type:
- Jump Infantry

Wargear:
- Power armour
- Bolt pistol
- The Blood Crozius
- Frag and krak grenades
- Jump Pack
- Rosarius

Special Rules:
- Descent of Angels
- The Black Rage
- Fearless
- Feel No Pain
- Furious Charge
- Fury Unbound
- Liturgies of Blood
- Relentless

TROOPS

DEATH COMPANY DREADNOUGHT ....125 Points

Page 29

You can include one Death Company Dreadnought for every five Death Company models in your army.

	WS	BS	S	F	S	R	I	A
Dreadnought	5	4	6	12	12	10	4	3(4)

(Armour: F, S, R)

Unit Composition:
- 1 Dreadnought

Unit Type:
- Vehicle (Walker)

Wargear:
- Blood fist with built-in storm bolter
- Blood fist with built-in meltagun
- Smoke launchers

Special Rules:
- Fleet
- Furious Charge
- None Can Stay My Wrath
- Rage

Options:
- Replace storm bolter with heavy flamer: ....+10 pts
- Replace both blood fists with a pair of blood talons (the built-in weapons are retained): ....free
- Take a magna-grapple ....+15 pts
- Take searchlight ....+1 pt

Dedicated Transport:
- Can select a Drop Pod (see page 90).

SCOUT SQUAD ....75 Points

Page 31

	WS	BS	S	T	W	I	A	Ld	Sv
Scout	3	3	4	4	1	4	1	8	4+
Scout Sergeant	4	4	4	4	1	4	2	9	4+

Unit Composition:
- 4 Scouts
- 1 Scout Sergeant

Unit Type:
- Infantry

Wargear:
- Scout armour
- Shotgun
- Bolt pistol
- Frag and krak grenades

Special Rules:
- And They Shall Know No Fear
- Combat Squads
- The Red Thirst
- Infiltrate
- Move Through Cover
- Scouts

Options:
- Add up to five Scouts ....+13 pts per model
- Any model can replace his shotgun with:
  - a boltgun, combat blade or sniper rifle ....free
- One Scout can replace his shotgun with:
  a heavy bolter or a missile launcher ....+10 pts
- The Scout Sergeant can replace his shotgun and/or bolt pistol with:
  - a combi-melta, -flamer or -plasma ....+10 pts
  - a plasma pistol or a power weapon.............+15 pts
  - a power fist ....+25 pts
- The Scout Sergeant can take:
  - melta bombs ....+5 pts
  - a locator beacon ....+25 pts
- The entire squad can have camo cloaks ....+3 pts per model

---

ASSAULT SQUAD ....100 Points

Page 25

	WS	BS	S	T	W	I	A	Ld	Sv
Space Marine	4	4	4	4	1	4	1	8	3+
Space Marine Sergeant	4	4	4	4	1	4	2	9	3+

Unit Composition:
- 4 Space Marines
- 1 Space Marine Sergeant

Unit Type:
- Jump infantry

Wargear:
- Power armour
- Bolt pistol
- Chainsword
- Frag and krak grenades
- Jump pack

Special Rules:
- Descent of Angels
- And They Shall Know No Fear
- Combat Squads
- The Red Thirst

Dedicated Transport:
- The squad can remove its jump packs to count as Infantry. It can then have any Dedicated Transport at a 35-point discount (see page 90)

Options:
- Add up to five Space Marines: ....+18 pts per model
- For every five models in the squad, one Space Marine can replace his bolt pistol with one of the following:
  - a flamer ....+5 pts per model
  - a meltagun or hand flamer ....+10 pts per model
  - a plasma gun/pistol or infernus pistol ..+15 pts per model
- The Sergeant can replace his bolt pistol/chainsword with:
  - a hand flamer ....+10 pts
  - a plasma pistol, infernus pistol, power weapon or lightning claw ....+15 pts
  - a storm shield ....+20 pts
  - a power fist ....+25 pts
  - a thunder hammer ....+30 pts
- The Space Marine Sergeant can take:
  - melta bombs ....+5 pts
  - a combat shield ....+5 pts

DEDICATED TRANSPORTS

Certain Space Marine units have the option of selecting a dedicated transport vehicle. These vehicles do not use up any Force Organisation chart selections, but otherwise function as separate units. See the Vehicles section of the Warhammer 40,000 rulebook for details of how transport vehicles operate.

RHINO .... 50 Points   Page 34

	BS	F	S	R
⌐ Armour ¬				
Rhino	4	11	11	10

Unit Composition:
• 1 Rhino

Transport Capacity:
• Ten models

Unit Type:
• Vehicle (Tank, Fast)

Special Rules:
• Repair

Wargear:
• Storm bolter
• Smoke launchers

Options:
• Can take any of the following:
  - a storm bolter ....+10 pts
  - a hunter-killer missile ....+10 pts
  - a dozer blade ....+5 pts
  - extra armour ....+15 pts
  - searchlight ....+1 pt

RAZORBACK .... 55 Points   Page 35

	BS	F	S	R
⌐ Armour ¬				
Razorback	4	11	11	10

Unit Composition:
• 1 Razorback

Transport Capacity:
• Six models

Unit Type:
• Vehicle (Tank, Fast)

Wargear:
• Twin-linked heavy bolter
• Smoke launchers

Options:
• Replace twin-linked heavy bolters with:
  - twin-linked heavy flamer ....free
  - twin-linked assault cannon ....+35 pts
  - twin-linked lascannon ....+35 pts
  - lascannon and twin-linked plasma gun ....+35 pts
• Can take any of the following:
  - a storm bolter ....+10 pts
  - a hunter-killer missile ....+10 pts
  - a dozer blade ....+5 pts
  - extra armour ....+15 pts
  - searchlight ....+1 pt

DROP POD .... 35 Points   Page 32

	BS	F	S	R
⌐ Armour ¬				
Drop Pod	4	12	12	12

Unit Composition:
• 1 Drop Pod

Transport Capacity:
• Ten models or
  one Dreadnought

Unit Type:
• Vehicle (Open-topped)

Special Rules:
• Inertial Guidance System
• Immobile
• Drop Pod Assault

Wargear:
• Storm bolter

Options:
• Replace storm bolter with
  deathwind missile launcher ....+20 pts
• Take a locator beacon ....+10 pts

DEDICATED TRANSPORTS

LAND RAIDER .... 250 Points

Page 37

	⌐ Armour ⌐		
	BS	F	S	R
Land Raider	4	14	14	14

Unit Composition:
• 1 Land Raider

Transport Capacity
• Ten models

Unit Type:
• Vehicle (Tank)

Special Rules:
• Assault Vehicle
• Deep Strike
• Power of the Machine Spirit

Wargear:
• Twin-linked heavy bolter
• Two twin-linked lascannons
• Smoke launchers

Options:
• Can take any of the following:
  - a storm bolter .... +10 pts
  - a hunter-killer missile .... +10 pts
  - a multi-melta .... +10 pts
  - extra armour .... +15 pts
  - searchlight .... +1 pt

LAND RAIDER CRUSADER .... 250 Points

Page 37

	⌐ Armour ⌐		
	BS	F	S	R
Land Raider	4	14	14	14

Unit Composition:
• 1 Land Raider

Transport Capacity
• Sixteen models

Unit Type:
• Vehicle (Tank)

Special Rules:
• Assault Vehicle
• Deep Strike
• Power of the Machine Spirit

Wargear:
• Twin-linked assault cannon
• Two hurricane bolters
• Frag assault launchers
• Smoke launchers

Options:
• Can take any of the following:
  - a storm bolter .... +10 pts
  - a hunter-killer missile .... +10 pts
  - a multi-melta .... +10 pts
  - extra armour .... +15 pts
  - searchlight .... +1 pt

LAND RAIDER REDEEMER .... 240 Points

Page 37

	⌐ Armour ⌐		
	BS	F	S	R
Land Raider	4	14	14	14

Unit Composition:
• 1 Land Raider

Transport Capacity
• Twelve models

Unit Type:
• Vehicle (Tank)

Special Rules:
• Assault Vehicle
• Deep Strike
• Power of the Machine Spirit

Wargear:
• Twin-linked assault cannon
• Two flamestorm cannons
• Frag assault launchers
• Smoke launchers

Options:
• Can take any of the following:
  - a storm bolter .... +10 pts
  - a hunter-killer missile .... +10 pts
  - a multi-melta .... +10 pts
  - extra armour .... +15 pts
  - searchlight .... +1 pt

FAST ATTACK

VANGUARD VETERAN SQUAD ....115 Points   Page 27

	WS	BS	S	T	W	I	A	Ld	Sv
Veteran	4	4	4	4	1	4	2	9	3+
Space Marine Sergeant	4	4	4	4	1	4	2	9	3+

Unit Composition:
- 1 Space Marine Sergeant
- 4 Veterans

Unit Type:
- Infantry

Wargear:
- Power armour
- Bolt pistol
- Chainsword
  (the Sergeant has a
  power sword instead).
- Frag and krak grenades

Special Rules:
- And They Shall
  Know No Fear
- Combat Squads
- The Red Thirst
- Heroic Intervention

Dedicated Transport:
- If the squad does not
  have jump packs, it can
  select any dedicated
  transport (see page 90).

Options:
- Add up to five Veterans ....+20 pts per model
- The entire squad can have jump packs ..+10 pts per model
- Any model can replace his bolt pistol
  and/or chainsword with:
  - a hand flamer ....+10 pts per model
  - a plasma pistol, infernus pistol,
    lightning claw or power weapon ......+15 pts per model
  - a storm shield ....+20 pts per model
  - a power fist ....+25 pts per model
  - a thunder hammer ....+30 pts per model
- Any model can take:
  - melta bombs ....+5 pts per model
- The Sergeant can replace his power sword with:
  - a lightning claw or Glaive Encarmine ....free
  - a power fist ....+10 pts
  - a thunder hammer ....+15 pts

LAND SPEEDER SQUADRON ....50 Points per model   Page 33

	┌ Armour ┐		
	BS	F	S	R
Land Speeder	4	10	10	10

Unit Composition:
- 1-3 Land Speeders

Unit Type:
- Vehicle (Fast, Skimmer)

Wargear:
- Heavy bolter

Special Rules:
- Deep Strike

Options:
- Any Land Speeder can replace its heavy bolter with:
  - heavy flamer ....free
  - multi-melta ....+10 pts pts per model
- Any Land Speeder can be upgraded with one of the
  following:
  - a Typhoon missile launcher ....+40 pts per model
  - a Tornado pattern:
    - heavy flamer or heavy bolter ....+10 pts
    - multi-melta ....+20 pts
    - assault cannon ....+40 pts

BAAL PREDATOR ....115 Points   Page 36

	┌ Armour ┐		
	BS	F	S	R
Baal Predator	4	13	11	10

Unit Composition:
- 1 Baal Predator

Unit Type:
- Vehicle (Tank, Fast)

Wargear:
- Twin-linked assault cannon
- Smoke launchers

Special Rules:
- Scouts

Options:
- Replace twin-linked assault cannon with:
  - a flamestorm cannon ....free
- Can take side sponsons with:
  - heavy flamers ....+25 pts
  - heavy bolters ....+30 pts
- Can take any of the following:
  - a storm bolter ....+10 pts
  - a hunter-killer missile ....+10 pts
  - a dozer blade ....+5 pts
  - extra armour ....+15 pts
  - searchlight ....+1 pt

FAST ATTACK

ATTACK BIKE SQUAD ....40 Points per model

Page 30

	WS	BS	S	T	W	I	A	Ld	Sv
Attack Bike	4	4	4	4(5)	2	4	2	8	3+

Unit Composition:
- 1-3 Attack Bikes

Unit Type:
- Bikes

Wargear:
- Power armour
- Heavy bolter
- Bolt pistol
- Frag and krak grenades
- Space Marine Bike

Special Rules:
- And They Shall Know No Fear
- The Red Thirst

Options:
- Any Attack Bike can upgrade its heavy bolter to a multi-melta ....+10 pts per model

BIKE SQUAD ....90 Points

Page 30

	WS	BS	S	T	W	I	A	Ld	Sv
Space Marine Biker	4	4	4	4(5)	1	4	1	8	3+
Biker Sergeant	4	4	4	4(5)	1	4	2	9	3+
Attack Bike	4	4	4	4(5)	2	4	2	8	3+

Unit Composition:
- 1 Biker Sergeant
- 2 Space Marine Bikers

Unit Type:
- Bikes

Wargear:
- Power armour
- Bolt pistol
- Frag and krak grenades
- Space Marine Bike

Special Rules:
- And They Shall Know No Fear
- Combat Squads
- The Red Thirst

Options:
- Add up to five Space Marine Bikers ......+25 pts per model
- The Biker Sergeant can replace his bolt pistol with:
  - a plasma pistol or power weapon ....+15 pts
  - a combi-melta, -flamer or -plasma ....+10 pts
  - a power fist ....+25 pts
- The Biker Sergeant can take melta bombs ....+5 pts
- Up to two Bikers can replace their bolt pistols with:
  - a flamer ....+5 pts per model
  - a meltagun ....+10 pts per model
  - a plasma gun ....+15 pts per model
- Add one Attack Bike to the Bike Squad................+40 pts
  - Upgrade the Attack Bike's heavy bolter to a multi-melta ....+10 pts

SCOUT BIKE SQUAD ....70 Points

Page 31

	WS	BS	S	T	W	I	A	Ld	Sv
Scout Biker	3	3	4	4(5)	1	4	1	8	4+
Scout Biker Sergeant	4	4	4	4(5)	1	4	2	9	4+

Unit Composition:
- 1 Scout Biker Sergeant
- 2 Scout Bikers

Unit Type:
- Bikes

Wargear:
- Scout armour
- Shotgun
- Bolt pistol
- Frag and krak grenades
- Space Marine bike

Special Rules:
- And They Shall Know No Fear
- Combat Squads
- The Red Thirst
- Infiltrate
- Scouts

Options:
- Add up to seven Scout Bikers ....+20 pts per model
- The Scout Biker Sergeant can replace his bolt pistol with:
  - a plasma pistol or power weapon ....+15 pts
  - a combi-melta, -flamer or -plasma ....+10 pts
  - a power fist ....+25 pts
- The Scout Biker Sergeant can take:
  - melta bombs ....+5 pts
  - locator beacon ....+25 pts
- Up to three Bikers can replace their bike's twin-linked boltgun with an Astartes grenade launcher ....+10 pts
- The squad can have cluster mines ....+10 pts
Note that a squad that separates into two Combat squads is still only treated as a single unit for the purposes of using cluster mines.

HEAVY SUPPORT

DREADNOUGHT ....105 Points   Page 29

	WS	BS	S	F	S	R	I	A
				⌐ Armour ¬				
Dreadnought	4	4	6	12	12	10	4	2

Unit Composition:
- 1 Dreadnought

Unit Type:
- Vehicle (Walker)

Wargear:
- Multi-melta
- Blood fist with built-in storm bolter
- Smoke launchers

Special Rules:
- The Red Thirst

Dedicated Transport:
- Can select a Drop Pod (see page 90).

Options:
- Replace storm bolter with heavy flamer: ....+10 pts
- Replace multi-melta with:
  - twin-linked heavy flamer ....free
  - twin-linked heavy bolter ....+5 pts
  - twin-linked autocannon ....+10 pts
  - plasma cannon or assault cannon ....+10 pts
  - twin-linked lascannon ....+30 pts
- Replace blood fist with:
  - twin-linked autocannon or missile launcher ......+5 pts
- Take extra armour ....+15 pts
- Take searchlight ....+1 pt

STORMRAVEN GUNSHIP ....200 Points   Page 38

	BS	F	S	R
		⌐ Armour ¬		
Stormraven	4	12	12	12

Unit Composition:
- 1 Stormraven

Unit Type:
- Vehicle (Fast, Skimmer)

Wargear:
- Twin-linked heavy bolter
- Twin-linked assault cannon
- Four bloodstrike missiles
- Ceramite Plating

Transport Capacity
- Twelve models and/or one Dreadnought

Special Rules:
- Assault Vehicle
- Deep Strike
- Power of the Machine Spirit
- Skies of Blood

Options:
- Replace twin-linked heavy bolter with:
  - twin-linked multi-melta ....free
  - typhoon missile launcher ....+25 pts
- Replace twin-linked assault cannon with:
  - twin-linked plasma cannon ....free
  - twin-linked lascannons ....free
- Can take side sponsons with hurricane bolters ......+30 pts
- Can take any of the following:
  - searchlight ....+1 pt
  - locator beacon ....+15 pts
  - extra armour ....+15 pts

PREDATOR ....70 Points   Page 35

	BS	F	S	R
		⌐ Armour ¬		
Predator	4	13	11	10

Unit Composition:
- 1 Predator

Unit Type:
- Vehicle (Tank, Fast)

Wargear:
- Autocannon
- Smoke launchers

Options:
- Replace autocannon with:
  - a twin-linked lascannon ....+45 pts
- Can take side sponsons with:
  - heavy bolters ....+30 pts
  - lascannons ....+65 pts
- Can take any of the following:
  - a storm bolter and/or a hunter-killer missile ....+10 pts
  - a dozer blade ....+5 pts
  - extra armour ....+15 pts
  - searchlight ....+1 pt

HEAVY SUPPORT

DEVASTATOR SQUAD .... 90 Points

	WS	BS	S	T	W	I	A	Ld	Sv
Space Marine	4	4	4	4	1	4	1	8	3+
Space Marine Sergeant	4	4	4	4	1	4	2	9	3+

Unit Composition:
- 4 Space Marines
- 1 Space Marine Sergeant

Unit Type:
- Infantry

Wargear:
- Power armour
- Boltgun
- Bolt pistol
- Frag and krak grenades
- The Sergeant also has a Signum

Special Rules:
- And They Shall Know No Fear
- Combat Squads
- The Red Thirst

Dedicated Transport:
- The squad can select any dedicated transport (see page 90).

Options:
- Add up to five Space Marines .... *+16 pts per model*
- Up to four Space Marines can replace their boltguns with one of the following:
  - a heavy bolter, multi-melta or a missile launcher .... *+10 pts per model*
  - a plasma cannon .... *+15 pts per model*
  - a lascannon .... *+25 pts per model*
- The Space Marine Sergeant can replace his boltgun and/or bolt pistol with:
  - a chainsword .... *free*
  - a storm bolter .... *+3 pts*
  - a combi-melta, -flamer or -plasma .... *+10 pts*
  - a plasma pistol or power weapon .... *+15 pts*
  - a power fist .... *+25 pts*
- The Space Marine Sergeant can take:
  - melta bombs .... *+5 pts*

VINDICATOR .... 145 Points

		Armour		
	BS	F	S	R
Vindicator	4	13	11	10

Unit Composition:
- 1 Vindicator

Unit Type:
- Vehicle (Tank, Fast)

Wargear:
- Demolisher cannon
- Storm bolter
- Smoke launchers

Options:
- Can take any of the following:
  - a storm bolter .... *+10 pts*
  - a hunter-killer missile .... *+10 pts*
  - a dozer blade .... *+5 pts*
  - a siege shield .... *+10 pts*
  - extra armour .... *+15 pts*
  - searchlight .... *+1 pt*

WHIRLWIND .... 90 Points

		Armour		
	BS	F	S	R
Whirlwind	4	11	11	10

Unit Composition:
- 1 Whirlwind

Unit Type:
- Vehicle (Tank, Fast)

Wargear:
- Whirlwind multiple missile launcher
- Smoke launchers

Options:
- Can take any of the following:
  - a storm bolter .... *+10 pts*
  - a hunter-killer missile .... *+10 pts*
  - a dozer blade .... *+5 pts*
  - extra armour .... *+15 pts*
  - searchlight .... *+1 pt*

SUMMARY

TROOP TYPES

	WS	BS	S	T	W	I	A	Ld	Sv	Page
Astorath the Grim	6	5	4	4	3	5	3	10	2+	45
Attack Bike	4	4	4	4(5)	2	4	2	8	3+	30
Biker Sergeant	4	4	4	4(5)	1	4	2	9	3+	30
Blood Champion	5	4	4	4	1	4	2	9	3+	52
Captain	6	5	4	4	3	5	3	10	3+	40
Captain Tycho	6	5	4	4	3	5	3	10	2+	41
Chaplain	5	4	4	4	2	4	2	10	3+	42
Commander Dante	6	5	4	4	4	6	4	10	2+	53
Corbulo	5	5	4	4	2	5	3	9	3+	49
Death Company	5	4	4	4	1	4	2	8	3+	44
Death Company Tycho	7	4	4	4	3	5	4	8	2+	41
Gabriel Seth	6	5	4	4	4	5	4	10	3+	55
Honour Guard	4	4	4	4	1	4	2	9	3+	52
Lemartes	5	4	4	4	2	6	2	10	3+	43
Librarian	5	4	4	4	2	4	2	10	3+	46
Mephiston	7	5	6	6	5	7	4	10	2+	47
Reclusiarch	5	5	4	4	3	5	3	10	3+	42
Sanguinary Guard	4	4	4	4	1	4	2	10	2+	50
Sanguinary Novitiate	4	4	4	4	1	4	2	9	3+	52
Sanguinary Priest	5	4	4	4	1	4	2	9	3+	48
The Sanguinor	8	5	5	4	3	6	5	10	2+	51
Scout Biker	3	3	4	4(5)	1	4	1	8	4+	31
Scout Biker Sergeant	4	4	4	4(5)	1	4	2	9	4+	31
Scout	3	3	4	4	1	4	1	8	4+	31
Scout Sergeant	4	4	4	4	1	4	2	9	4+	31
Servitor	3	3	3	3	1	3	1	8	4+	39
Space Marine	4	4	4	4	1	4	1	8	3+	24
Space Marine Biker	4	4	4	4(5)	1	4	1	8	3+	30
Space Marine Sergeant	4	4	4	4	1	4	2	9	3+	24
Techmarine	4	4	4	4	1	4	1	8	2+	39
Terminator	4	4	4	4	1	4	2	9	2+	28
Terminator Sergeant	4	4	4	4	1	4	2	9	2+	28
Veteran	4	4	4	4	1	4	2	9	3+	27

VEHICLES

	BS	Front	Side	Rear	Page
		Armour			
Baal Predator	4	13	11	10	36
Drop Pod	4	12	12	12	32
Land Raider	4	14	14	14	37
Land Speeder	4	10	10	10	33
Predator	4	13	11	10	35
Razorback	4	11	11	10	35
Rhino	4	11	11	10	34
Stormraven	4	12	12	12	38
Vindicator	4	13	11	10	35
Whirlwind	4	11	11	10	35

	WS	BS	S	Front	Side	Rear	I	A	Page
				Armour					
Death Company Dreadnought	5	4	6	12	12	10	4	3(4)	29
Dreadnought	4	4	6	12	12	10	4	2	29
Furioso Dreadnought	6	4	6	13	12	10	4	2(3)	29

WEAPON TYPES

Weapon	Range	Str.	AP	Type	Page
Angelus Boltgun	12"	4	4	Assault 2	50
Assault Cannon	24"	6	4	Heavy 4, Rending	56
Astartes Grenade Launcher*					56
(Frag)	24"	3	6	Rapid Fire, Blast	
(Krak)	24"	6	4	Rapid Fire	
Autocannon	48"	7	4	Heavy 2	60
Bloodstrike Missiles	72"	8	1	Heavy 1, One shot	38
Boltgun	24"	4	5	Rapid Fire	56
Bolt Pistol	12"	4	5	Pistol	56
Cyclone Missile Launcher*					56
(Frag)	48"	4	6	Heavy 2, Blast	
(Krak)	48"	8	3	Heavy 2	
Deathwind Launcher	12"	5	-	Heavy1, Large Blast	32
Demolisher Cannon	24"	10	2	Ordnance 1	60
Flamer	Template	4	5	Assault 1	57
Flamestorm Cannon	Template	6	3	Heavy 1	36
Frag Cannon	Template	6	-	Assault 2, Rending	60
Hand Flamer	Template	3	6	Pistol	57
Heavy Bolter	36"	5	4	Heavy 3	57
Heavy Flamer	Template	5	4	Assault 1	57
Infernus Pistol	6"	8	1	Pistol, Melta	57
Lascannon	48"	9	2	Heavy 1	57
Magna-Grapple*	12"	8	2	Heavy 1, Grapple	60
Meltagun	12"	8	1	Assault 1, Melta	57
Missile Launcher*					58
(Frag)	48"	4	6	Heavy 1, Blast	
(Krak)	48"	8	3	Heavy 1	
Multi-melta	24"	8	1	Heavy 1, Melta	58
Plasma Cannon	36"	7	2	Heavy 1, Blast, Gets Hot!	58
Plasma Gun	24"	7	2	Rapid Fire, Gets Hot!	58
Plasma Pistol	12"	7	2	Pistol, Gets Hot!	58
Shotgun	12"	4	-	Assault 2	58
Sniper Rifle	36"	X	6	Heavy 1, Sniper	58
Storm Bolter	24"	4	5	Assault 2	58
Typhoon Missile Launcher*					33
(Frag)	48"	4	6	Heavy 2, Blast	
(Krak)	48"	8	3	Heavy 2	
Whirlwind Multiple Missile Launcher*					61
(Vengeance Missiles)	12-48"	5	4	Ordnance 1, Barrage	
(Incendiary Castellan Missiles)	12-48"	4	5	Ordnance1, Barrage, Ignores cover	

* These weapons have additional rules (see the relevant entry).

> "No hymn can be so uplifting
> as the roar of these guns."
>
> – Sergeant Ferato, Armourer